Personal FINANCE

DANTES/DSST* Study Guide

All rights reserved. This Study Guide, Book and Flashcards are protected under the US Copyright Law. No part of this book or study guide or flashcards may be reproduced, distributed or stored in a retrieval system, or transmitted in any form or by any means, electronic, mechanical, photocopying, recording, or otherwise, without the prior written permission of the publisher Breely Crush Publishing, LLC.

© 2019 Breely Crush Publishing, LLC

*DSST is a registered trademark of The Thomson Corporation and its affiliated companies, and does not endorse this book.

971092217143

Copyright ©2003 - 2019, Breely Crush Publishing, LLC.

All rights reserved.

This Study Guide, Book and Flashcards are protected under the US Copyright Law. No part of this publication may be reproduced, distributed or stored in a retrieval system, or transmitted in any form or by any means, electronic, mechanical, photocopying, recording, or otherwise, without the prior written permission of the publisher Breely Crush Publishing, LLC.

Published by Breely Crush Publishing, LLC
10808 River Front Parkway
South Jordan, UT 84095
www.breelycrushpublishing.com

ISBN-10: 1-61433-605-9
ISBN-13: 978-1-61433-605-1

Printed and bound in the United States of America.

DSST is a registered trademark of The Thomson Corporation and its affiliated companies, and does not endorse this book.

Table of Contents

Introduction 1
Chapter 1 - The Fundamentals 4
Inflation and the Value of Money 6
Money Supply 6
Time Value of Money 7
The Consumer Price Index 8
Personal Budgeting and Planning 9
Key Budgeting Strategy 11
Setting Financial Goals 11
Personal Financial Statement and Net Worth 12
Personal Financial Statement 15
Cash Flow Management: Where Did the Money Go? 17
Economic Terminology 18
Sample Test Questions - Chapter 1 21
Chapter 2 - Credit and Debit 26
Secured and Unsecured Credit 28
Credit Cards 30
Interest Rates 30
Types of Interest 31
How Interest Rates Are Determined 31
Institutional Loan Evaluation and Interest Rate Fixing Process Flow 32
Credit Scores and Credit Reporting 32
FICO Scores 33
Seven Year Records 33
Credit Repair 34
Bankruptcy 35
Too Much Credit 36
Sample Test Questions - Chapter 2 37
Chapter 3 - Let's Go Shopping! 43
Truth In Lending and The Consumer Protection Agency 43
The Home 43
The Process of Purchasing a Home 44
The FSBO Process 46
First Time Home Buyers Tax Credit 46
Fixed and Adjustable Rate Mortgages 47
Front Loaded Interest 47
Accelerated Mortgage Pay-Down Strategy 48
Car Purchase 48
Upside Down and Underwater 50
Leasing a Car 51
Education 51
Time Value of Money and Planning for Your Children's College Fund 51

Financial Aid for Higher Education	*52*
Grants, Scholarships and Fellowships	*53*
The Federal Pell Grant	*53*
Student Loans and Sallie Mae	*53*
Private Loans	*54*
Loan Forgiveness Programs	*54*
Military Educational Benefits	*54*
Make Your Own Scholarship	*55*
Sample Test Questions - Chapter 3	*56*
Chapter 4 - Taxes	*61*
Income Taxes	*61*
W-2 Status	*62*
1099 Status	*62*
Other Payroll Taxes	*63*
April 15th	*63*
Estimated Taxes	*64*
Sample Test Questions - Chapter 4	*65*
Chapter 5 - Financial Planning	*71*
Creating Wealth	*71*
The Power of Tax Free Compounding Investment	*72*
Establishing Financial Priorities	*72*
Budgeting Considerations	*73*
Life Insurance	*74*
Liability Insurance	*74*
Disability Insurance	*75*
COBRA	*75*
HIPAA	*76*
Medical Insurance	*76*
Emergency Living Expenses	*76*
Investing Overview	*78*
The Risk-Reward Pyramid	*78*
Typical Goals and Investment Vehicles	*79*
Typical Investing Model For Success	*81*
Sample Test Questions - Chapter 5	*83*
Chapter 6 - Retirement Plans and Estate Planning	*89*
Personal Pension Planning	*91*
401k Pension Plan	*91*
Individual Retirement Account - IRA	*93*
Estate Planning	*95*
Sample Test Questions - Chapter 6	*97*
Sample Test Questions - Overview	*103*
Test Taking Strategies	*109*
Test Preparation	*109*
Legal Note	*110*

Introduction

As a citizen of the modern world, we are in large part economic entities. We consume and we produce. In that process, we all play an important part in the complex economic web that has allowed our species to multiply and prosper. Individuals, corporations as well as entire nations can abuse the system and can produce a mysterious, intangible, creeping malaise that can have direct and disastrous consequences for those unlucky enough to be in the wrong place at the wrong time. Highly educated professionals trained in the black arts of finance and economics try to read the entrails of sophisticated computer models but the "laws" of finance and economics still seem to be beyond the reach of total control. Indeed, some modern era philosophers espouse the idea that capitalism is a deal made with the devil. The argument goes that if one's life style or success depends mainly on a beneficent cash flow from a third party, there can be the tendency to rationalize decisions and actions to maintain that life giving flow at almost any cost. Corruption, deceit and cold ruthlessness casts a pall on the good that enlightened self- interest can bring. But it may very well just come with the territory.

But too many innocent bystanders become collateral damage to the vagaries of a complex system gone off course. It's an unfortunate truth that much of the lifestyle and self-image a modern citizen has can depend heavily on the job and the cash flow it produces. If for some reason, that cash flow becomes cut-off; a modern day tragedy of events can befall the unfortunate victim. Fortunately, that event becomes less likely as the economy sails on smooth waters. But there are always economic storms lurking out there on the horizon and intelligent and experienced participants understand the need for being prepared for the potential storms always lurking just beyond the horizon- ready to strike when you least expect it.

Ironically, the benefits of a productive economic system can become the siren's song for over consumption and risky financial behavior. In today's consumer based capitalism, credit is that siren's song. The seduction of marketing combined with the enabler of easy credit can be a formula for financial ruin and tremendous daily stress. For those many unfortunate debtors who have been brought up with the traditional values of responsibility and social cooperation, being in serious debt can turn the word freedom into self-imposed slavery. Working two and three jobs, not having time to smell the roses and cold digital credit scores can become the signposts of failure and can weigh heavily on the private lives of modern, over-extended consumers.

The tragedy is often caused by poor choices on the part of decision makers at the top of the chain of responsibility or events well beyond the control of the workers who suffer the consequences. Even though events totally out of a workers control can come home to roost on the innocent in the form of a pink slip, in a free, capitalistic system it is still up to the individual to prepare for the consequences-be it just or unjust.

Unfortunately, insult is added to injury can come tumbling down when excessive impulse buying and easy credit come together in an event of unfortunate timing in the form of disappearing income and mounting bills. Each call from the credit collectors feels like a slap in the face and the unfortunate unemployed worker can begin to feel like a "loser." Soon, the worker can begin to believe it. The worker's spirit, once riding high on false pride in the superficial things purchased and displayed to the world as who that person is now represent the naive folly of thinking it could never happen to them. After all, playing by the rules is no guarantee from disaster. Bitterness and despair can flood into not only a person's life but the also the innocent family as well. Indeed, being unemployed in a society of abundance can become a difficult test in many subtle ways. Millions suffer daily from this modern economic-social injustice. Yes, capitalism is all about risk and reward, but the reality is that sometimes it is all about the risk. And being an employee for even the most powerful corporations or even the government is no guarantee that cost cutting (risk for the employee) won't be put into effect by those who can only pretend to sympathize. In fact, this is most likely to happen when a young employee is just starting out and on the bottom of the seniority list. In recent times, recessions have been infrequent and layoffs have been relatively fee-until recently. When economic times are good, rainy day thinking takes a back seat. Indeed, it should never take a back seat. And that is one of the main reasons for this book; as the old saying goes: "Fore warned is fore armed."

Unfortunately, in today's modern society, most parents and educational systems don't do a very good job of educating upcoming generations on finance and economics. It appears that the attitude is "sink or swim."

In all fairness, most parents are focused on working hard just to pay bills and living from day-to- day. Where do the younger generations turn for an example of how to manage finances? Is it their parents who are most likely constantly stressed out over making ends meet? Is it the local or federal governments who constantly develop budgets only to violate them with impunity? What are the rules for economic survival?
In the American society where almost seventy percent (70%) of the nation's gross national product depends on consumption, how do we instill the idea of deferred gratification and personal fiscal responsibility? Sadly, easy credit and powerful marketing can make for a risky lifestyle and become overly dependent on immediate cash flow. Not many people mention the fact that perhaps the powerful squeeze between debt and the need for immediate cash flow has fostered and legitimized corruption and weak values. The facts seem to lead to the rather depressing conclusion that many important business and financial decisions are made by people who may have their personal backs up against the financial wall and make decisions based upon how the outcome will affect their own personal situations. Unfortunately, making the "right" decision can at times be synonymous with financial suicide. Indeed, this unfortunate fact of dependency may be the cause for the growing number of absurd public and private decisions and events.

Most modern day Americans intuitively understand the precarious lifestyles we have developed. But few seem to know how to correct the paradox of such stress and uncertainty suffered within the context of such abundance and opportunity. This book will attempt to provide the reader with a clear guide that will hopefully help change the modern way of building a personal financial house of cards as so many seem to do. It just takes some planning and discipline to make this marvelous system to work for you.

Did you know that it's fairly simple to become a millionaire? This encouraging fact becomes apparent when we move on to an important discussion of the effect of time on money and how that impacts investment and planning. Believe it or not, all it takes is a pinch of capital and a big measure of patience to become a millionaire. Sounds easy, doesn't it? But obviously, that is easier said than done. As most readers will be starting their adult lives, this section can have a tremendous impact on financial planning. Indeed, the magic of compounding can almost insure financial success when matched with discipline and patience.

Then we proceed to the important topic of that marvelous mechanism for progress and that most dangerous poison that feeds greed and materialism: credit. Make no mistake, capitalism in its current form depends heavily on credit, but too much of a good thing can become the rope that hangs the borrower. Indeed, Uncle Sam is currently looking up at the gallows. The solution is as simple as reading a financial statement.

Speaking of credit, we will move right on to the fun part – buying those big items that almost always involve financing. We will go over how to avoid the hype and make logical purchasing decisions based upon independent, objective information. Buying is a lot of fun, but it is always surrounded by hype and it is far more fun to know what you are buying before committing to the purchase. Purchasing should be a logical process and not an emotional roll of the dice. As a consumer goes through life, certain anecdotal rules come into play. "Rules" such as "expenses rise to meet income" or … "there is no such thing as a free lunch" have some validity and need to be recognized.

In a consumer society, the pressures are great to consume and so much consumption is made on an emotional level. There is a whole profession and industry dedicated to parting consumers from their money, whether or not they can afford it! Then the poor consumer can find themselves caught in the stressful squeeze of over consumption and under capitalization. Learning how to avoid that stressful situation is one of the main objectives of the book. Indeed, there are times to be a consumer and times not to be a consumer. Learning when to play the role needs to be clearly defined so that emotions can be put in context.

Next is the discussion of an important and controversial subject: taxes. Nothing is for certain except death and taxes but that doesn't mean that you don't need to do your homework. Indeed, taxation may become the central issue for the near future. Part of being a responsible citizen requires that there be payments made for the common good: aka, paying taxes. Taxes are a significant expense in all of our lives-if we are lucky. Indeed, if you are paying taxes you are making income! However, the role of taxes and the U.S. economy is perhaps the most intractable economic problem now facing the U.S. and the question begs itself: how will the U.S. resolve the long term debt and how this might impact your future tax bite (meaning will there be less disposable income?).

Today, many people think that personal financial success is defined by what a person can purchase. First, it's the car; then the house; the boat; a vacation home; exotic vacations and then …… This type of financial benchmarking is what we call day dreaming-nothing more. Real financial success begins with a plan that defines what a person wants, what needs to be done to get what you want and what you can reasonably expect to achieve. Successful personal finance is not about pie-in-the-sky but stands firmly grounded in cold, hard reality. Dreams and aspirations are only as good as their ability to be realized. With well researched planning and disciplined implementation, anything can be attained. Without knowledge, planning and discipline, a person usually ends up with what they are given. And that is not the best way to aspire to anything.

We Americans talk very easily about freedom and liberty, but becoming an economic slave to our own lack of knowledge and discipline can make freedom a hollow word. With freedom comes social, political and financial responsibilities and it begins, as in most things, with education.

As this book is being written, a once mighty nation is looking into the financial abyss and we need to change the irresponsible way we look upon credit and get back to solid, responsible thinking. And it starts with you.

The only reason a great many American families don't own an elephant is that they have never been offered an elephant for a dollar down and easy weekly payments.
~Mad Magazine

 Chapter 1 - The Fundamentals

At the heart of any economy is the method of exchange. Thousands of years ago, barter was the principal means for exchange. You would get four sheep for your wagon load of wheat. You traded the sheep for six pigs and so it went. As times changed and economies grew, it became inconvenient, cumbersome and dangerous to trade real goods, so civilization invented a safer and easier way for exchange: resentative value. Way back in the early Egyptian and Mesopotamian civilizations, business was transacted with promises to pay written out on clay tablets or papyrus. "I, Horgath of New Babylon, promise to exchange for the holder of this tablet six extra large clay storage vessels of quality pressed olive oil." Of course, acceptance of such a flimsy guarantee depended mainly on who issued the tablet. In today's modern economies, it is the government that guarantees that the method of exchange for everybody is "officially backed." Indeed, money, be it paper or digital, is just a promise to exchange the money for anything of equal value to be determined by the parties of each transaction. In other words, as long as the parties to the transaction agree that the money has value, exchanges can take place.

However, history has shown that governments are fallible and over the centuries collapsing governments were preceded by the collapse of their currencies. When currencies begin to fail, there is usually a stampede into other portable forms of value. Cigarettes, tools, firearms and any other portable and necessary items become temporary symbols of value. In today's world, most people prefer to hedge the loss of value in their local currencies by owning gold, silver or the currencies of other more stable countries. Since the end of World War II, the U.S. dollar has become the default currency due to the fact that up until recently, the U.S. dollar has been seen as the most secure and stable currency. Indeed, even today when chaos threatens, local currencies flee into the U.S. dollar. In fact, a nation's image of stability is almost directly correlated to the relative value of its currency to that of other nations.

In 1971, President Richard Nixon removed the U.S. dollar from the gold standard and set free the value of the dollar to the whims of perception. No longer could a dollar bill be exchanged for a certain fixed amount of gold or silver. The value of the paper was totally dependent on universal acceptance that the symbol (money) was a secure measure of exchange and that it would be universally accepted as having a specific value. So, today, we trade paper for just about everything. Some of the more skeptical citizens call unbacked currency as "fiat money." Indeed, in the modern global world, digits that fly at the speed of light from one account to another and this makes the world of commerce function. And the whole idea of transfer of wealth is built on a universal perception that the method of exchange has real value. It isn't money that makes the world go around…it's shared perception that a symbol has meaning. But let there be no doubt, without this mystical consensus, economies around the world would plunge into immediate chaos and terrible consequences would ensue. As a matter of fact, the recent financial crisis was a very serious test of confidence in the U.S. dollar. Indeed, it was another episode of irresponsible government and it has become obvious that key players-private and public- might very well force a drastic change in the world monetary system if they manage to shake our collective perception of the U.S. dollar. Given the fact that about once every decade, there appears some surprise crisis in the complex financial system, all citizens must be aware of the fragility and dependence of perception on which a modern economy is built.

Inflation and the Value of Money

Another important characteristic of money is that it constantly shrinks in value. Most obvious signs of the shrinkage happen when it takes more money to purchase the same goods. Often times, inflation is "creeping" and reveals itself in small increases in the price of goods and services. What causes this ever-present financial cancer?

Money Supply

Governments, usually in the form of a treasury department and central banks, are tasked with the job of producing and maintaining the value of their currencies. At the same time, governments are also tasked with the job of trying to promote a healthy economy. The real balancing act is between making money plentiful but not overly so. If too much money is put into circulation, it can become overly stimulative and citizens will feel "wealthy" and tend to spend freely. An increase in the supply of money can lead to an increase in prices as more and more people consume and put pressure on production. This "demand-push" prompts producers and others in the chain of production and distribution to feel that they can increase prices without hurting demand. In this case, the excess of money can create a general increase in demand and a resultant increase in prices. Of course, if there is too little currency in circulation, this can cause the opposite reaction and create a decrease in prices as demand falls; this is called deflation.

In general, the population of the world is constantly increasing; sometimes in spurts and sometimes at a steady rate; but the world's population is continuing to increase and is estimated to rise from the current 6 billion to 9 billion by 2050. To help provide for the growth in population, economies also need a growth in money supply.

As a result of this basic fact, governments with increasing populations need to constantly expand their money supply. Some structural inflation is a built in feature of the nature of money, particularly if there is no constraints on the ability of governments to fabricate the wonderful stuff. This institutionalized inflation makes it necessary to understand that over time, the value of money will erode.

For example: suppose you have deposited $10,000 in a zero interest paying savings account and there is an average annual inflation rate of 5% for the next 20 years. Over that time span, your savings account will become worth only $3,858 in today's money. This is called the **future value of money**. Another way to put it is that over the next twenty years, the value of future money loses over 60% of its present value. Stand it on its head and it means that if your salary is $50,000 today (present value), you would need a salary of about $125,000 (future value) to have the same purchasing power 20 years later. Of course, this doesn't include the fact that you would probably be paying higher income taxes on the higher salary. Except for rare and brief periods in modern history, inflation is always creeping up to suck the purchasing power from your money. That is why planning for the future is so important. Standing still economically is actually moving backwards.

Because of inflation and what it does to future value requires that present value of funds must be "put to work" to compensate for inflation over time. For example, if you want to have the same purchasing power of $10,000 that you have in your savings account today five years from now, you will need to earn at least enough income on your savings (interest) to cancel out the effects of inflation and the devaluation in purchasing power your savings would have in five years.

Let's look at an example: $10,000 today; average inflation rate for the next five years: 5%. Five years from now, your $10,000 will have a purchasing value of a relative $8,370. So, to preserve the purchasing power over the five years, you would need at least 5% interest income on your money (net of taxes and other expenses) to offset the effects of inflation. Or you can look at it another way: if you want to have $10,000 of purchasing power in today's value of goods and services and you have a zero interest rate savings account, you would need to have place $12,763 in your saving account to have the same purchasing power five years from now.

There is no need to go over the math involved in this exercise and there are plenty of online calculators. The important thing to keep in mind is that unless your accumulated wealth is somehow gaining in value, inflation will rob you so that you will have less tomorrow than you have today. At a minimum, all of your investments (passive income) should make, at a minimum, at least the projected rate of inflation. In this way, the future value of the present value will at least keep purchasing parity in the future. This is the general concept of Time Value of Money (TVM) and you will see that not only can this work against you, but it can be turned on its head and become a powerful ally.

 Time Value of Money

Suppose you want to know what the future value of an investment would be if you invested $10,000 today at an annual interest rate of 10% for 10 years? To find out what the real future value of the investment would be, you would need to deduct the estimated annual inflation rate from the interest rate to find a true estimated rate of return. So, in this case, if the forecast inflation rate is 3%, you would input 7% as the interest rate per time period. Also, you would need to consider other associated expenses such as taxes, commissions and fees. Are you surprised by the size of the increase in the investment? This is called the power of compounding interest and we will talk more about this important concept later in the study guide.

Of course, in the real world, most people just "cross the price bridges when they get there" and think of inflation as an act of nature. What do you think the odds are for that kind of planning to make things really happen as you would like? What do you think the odds are if you plan ahead as we just did? So, the real take away this example of the time value of money is that if you want to really achieve your goals, you need to plan ahead and be aware of the effects of time and inflation. Today's prices will with a high degree of probability be higher in the future. So, the income you receive to maintain the lifestyle you have today will need to be forever increasing just to stay up with core inflation.

The Consumer Price Index

Typically, governments price a number of goods that are representative of the normal purchases made by citizens in the local economy. This is called a "**market basket**." The cost of this basket is then compared over time. The results make up the **Consumer Price Index (CPI)**, which is the cost of the market basket today as a percentage of the cost of that identical basket at the start of the year. Sounds logical, doesn't it? But, the question begs itself: who chooses what items go into that basket? For example, before 1986, the market price for a barrel of oil was included in the formula. After the oil shocks of the '70s and early '80s, the volatile price of oil was taken out of the basket. The same thing happened to housing prices. Indeed, some of the items most important in the life of a consumer have been deleted from the basket and this can distort the "real" inflation rate faced by citizens. Indeed, the CPI also plays an important part in the cost of money in the form of interest rates.

To pay depositors for the use of their money and to at least cover the loss of value due to inflation, banks and other lending institutions must partially base the interest rates they must pay depositors on the government measure of inflation based mainly on the CPI. So, if inflation is low, banks pay low interest rates to compensate for the use of depositor funds. Today, there are many economists who feel that the real rate of inflation is more like 6% due to the costs of some important consumer items not included in the governments market basket; things like insurance, housing, medicines and educational costs. Again, it gets back to who decides what goes into the basket used to define the CPI. Why do we need to know this?

It gets back to the idea that the value of money and other key aspects of the modern economy depends largely on perception. For example, it the CPI remains low, the amount of interest a lender must pay depositors to lend out their deposits will remain low. This allows banks more on the "spread" between what the banks can borrow and what they can lend it out for. In the same fashion, if the banks pay very low interest rates to depositors, it forces more risky investing on the part of would be depositors as they seek a higher return. Given the divergence between the CPI and what the "real inflation rate" is, bank depositors are losing money putting funds in a bank. For example, if you open a savings account at your local bank, you are likely to earn only about 1.25% annual interest. This is well below the inflation rate. Of course, banks can offer other higher interest bearing investments but these usually require a higher risk tolerance and most likely provide banks with higher commissions.

Both the discussions of the Time Value of Money and inflation lead us to the concept of becoming a proactive member of the economy and protecting our own interests. Understanding just a few of the fundamentals can make a big difference in financial outcomes. For instance, look at your own consumption habits and how you spend money to help define what your own "real inflation rate" is. If you like to eat out a lot, your personal inflation rate may be much higher than others who don't. But how do you know your consumption patterns and your income needs? Let's meet the most important tool for the responsible consumer…the budget.

Personal Budgeting and Planning

For most people, knowing the truth of one's financial discipline has little appeal; ignorance is a good copout for irresponsible behavior. Even more difficult is to expect young people in the height of their spontaneous years to practice fiscal responsibility. Indeed, talking about budgeting is stogy stuff. However, being prudent and spontaneous are not mutually exclusive. Let's just say it's much more fun to be spontaneous and have some money than not.

Even though you might be a poor student dependent on generous donations from parents, part time jobs or a combination of both, not having much money makes it even more important to know where each cent is going. All economic beings in a monetary economy require some sort of income so they can consume the things they need.

There is little doubt that almost everybody knows what their income is but few know what their consumption is. Budgeting usually kicks in when the balance gets close to zero or the ATM says "insufficient funds." As a matter of fact, this empty pocket budgeting learned in adolescence and early adulthood too often carries on as a form of "intuitive budgeting" well into adulthood. Perhaps this fact is a result of never having any instruction on how to set up and stick to a budget.

Let's look at a simple student budget. We will consider that the student lives off campus and has a part time job working in a bookstore. Use this example to establish your own budget.

Income		
Parents	1000	
Bookstore	800	
Total Income	1800	
Expenses		
Rent		475
Food		600
Transportation		200
Utilities		60
Cell phone		30
Books and supplies		75
Laundry		30
Misc living exp.		150
Entertainment		180
Total Expenses		**1800**

What gives power to the process of setting up a budget is actually going through and analyzing what is consumed. The very act of seeing the numbers in front of you will help raise spending awareness.

Normally, it is better to use a system that allows a person to track each expenditure. Writing a check and coding the check to an expense category or using a debit card makes for easy tracking at the end of the month. But oftentimes, cash is still needed for some transactions. In which case, it is a good idea to write a separate check to Cash-Misc. Living Exp for those types of transactions that require the use cash. At the end of each month, numbers are transferred from the checkbook or debit card statements to the budget. This is usually set up on a spread sheet although there are many inexpensive budgeting software programs on the market (i.e., Quicken). The idea is to account and track variations from your planned budget. Even though you may think you don't make many transactions, you will be surprised. Besides, it's good discipline to sit down every month and do your budget because once it becomes a habit it will prove essential as your income and expenses expand after leaving student life.

 ## Key Budgeting Strategy

Once you establish a budget that reflects your consumption patterns, you will have a good idea of what your "disposable income" (income less expenses) might be. Once you know what portion of your income you can normally save, you should write a check for the disposable amount and put it into a liquid savings account at the time you receive have your maximum income for the month. In other words, don't make your disposable income what is leftover after your spending for the month. Discipline yourself to make your savings the first check you write, not the last. This will help you keep to your budget at the same time increasing your wealth and your future options. This is particularly important when you start to move up in your earning capacity.

 ## Setting Financial Goals

Once you have established a budget, you can do some planning…become financially proactive. Studies have shown that defining goals, ways to achieve them and writing it down provide a much higher success rate than just verbalizing what you would like to see happen. Each year, almost every business produces a business plan for the coming year. In fact, producing a business plan is so important that most companies mandate an annual plan. Creating a plan not only helps set up some expectations based on the perceived realities of the situation, but it also allows benchmarking progress toward the goals. So let's look at a typical financial plan for a young professional just out of university. The young graduate has an entry level job with a software development company. It is a small company and has no benefits such as health insurance, company retirement plan and other benefits usually offered by larger companies.

The financial plan begins with the identification of personal short and long term goals. This is followed by professional short and long term goals (long term means over five years from the date of the plan). If you don't have any goals, now is a good time to identify some.

Ironically, at eighteen or so, young people are supposed to have enough knowledge of themselves and the world around them to enable them to identify their chosen fields. This is usually a false premise. A good idea is to take some psychological profile and career aptitude tests like the MAPP or Strong Interest Inventory tests to see where a student's interests and personality would be a good match with a particular profession. Getting a formal education is an expensive proposition and it makes sense to do some research before committing the funds and the years of effort. Without a doubt, one of the best indicators of success is the happiness and fulfillment that a profession brings.

This is more important than mere financial reward. If you like something, you will be good at it.

Next, the plan focuses on identifying personal strengths and weaknesses and how to leverage and improve in the coming years. In the name of objectivity, it is a good idea to ask others who know you well and ask them to tell you the truth. It might hurt your feelings but it will help you improve. Nobody is perfect…or even close.

It is important at this point to realize that taxes can be a significant expense and need to be accounted for in the budget. Again, as a student, this may not be a factor as most will still be considered as dependents of the parents. If, however, you work to pay all your bills, you may need to file a tax return and pay taxes.

Once a budget has been established, look for your disposable income (income less all expenses) and decide how you would want to allocate the excess. Compare the disposable income with your short and long term goals. Then determine how using your disposable income could be used to help achieve some of your goals. As an ongoing process, at the end of each month take a look at the budget and see if there are expense categories that you can cut back on or substitute with other types of less expensive consumption.

For example, a student has a tendency to overspend on entertainment and that's to be expected. But if that amount is limited to discounted activities (happy hour, midnight movies, used books, special promotions, etc.) those savings can help add to other expense items or disposable income-assuming that entertainment is a budget item and not considered as disposable income. This action of evaluation, prioritizing and sizing is called "budgeting." Believe it or not, most people don't budget…they spend until they run out of money and then turn to the credit card to finance items (interest expense) that don't fit into the budget. Indeed, this sort of "budgeting" is what contributes to the growing number of personal bankruptcies (over 2 million annual personal bankruptcies and growing) and companies who find themselves in financial trouble (85% of companies fail after five years).

Personal Financial Statement and Net Worth

Seeking credit almost always requires the disclosure of the borrower's financial condition. The information provided provides a snapshot of the applicant's financial condition at that point in time. Among other things, a lender wants to know how the added loan payment, if approved, would affect the financial condition of the applicant and if the proposed loan meets certain requirements set by each individual lender.

The Personal Financial Statement provides a listing of the borrower's assets and liabilities to see what the net worth (assets less liabilities) of the individual is. An important thing to consider is that most credit cards and many types of debt can be "called in full" at any time. This means that the entire balance, not just the minimum payment, can be demanded to be paid in full before the term of the loan is reached. So, for most lenders, credit card debt is considered as an immediate debt even though the borrower does not see that effect on their available cash balance.

Recent history revealed that from 2005 until 2008, obtaining credit was as easy as showing up and demonstrating your ability to breathe. But once the credit crisis raised its ugly head, things have changed drastically. Indeed, the financial crisis was caused by a stunning loss of financial discipline from all parties concerned. Now, it's back to business as it was meant to be and was practiced for many decades. Loan officers once again look closely and verify financial information.

Example Personal Financial Plan

1. Personal Goals
    a) Short term (12 mos.)
    b) Long term (5 yrs.)
2. Professional or Educational Goals
    a) Short term (12 mos.)
    b) Long term (5 yrs.)
3. Personal Strengths
    a) How to improve and leverage
4. Personal Weaknesses
    a) How to improve
    b) Cost to improve (time and/or money)
    c) How to measure improvement
5. Things holding me back and how to overcome them

	Estimate	Actual	Over/Under	Notes
Income				
Source A				
Source B				
Total Income				
Expenses				
Housing				
Food				
Clothing				
Laundry dry cleaning				
Transportation				
Utilities				
Telephone - Cell				
Entertainment				
Education				
Insurance				
Pharmacy - Medical				
Miscellaneous				
Taxes				
Total Expenses				
Disposable Income (Income - Expenses)				
Savings				
Investements				
Other				

A budget is a simple tool that can make a major difference in your life. The American economy is set up to promote impulse buying. While the budget is no guarantee that you will follow it, just try it for several months and you will see how it makes you think first before pulling out your checkbook or credit card. That alone can save thousands of dollars each year. Budget line items should be conservative estimates and are not hard and fast. The line items shown are only examples and you may use any number and variation of line items needed to help define income and expenditures. The Yearly Plan budget is used for planning and not the working budget to be used on a monthly basis. The following budget is an example of a monthly budget.

If you use a check book, each line item should have a number and that number should be noted on each check so that the expense can be properly placed. The budget is only as good as its implementation and each line item should be analyzed for being over or under the budget estimate. The idea is to constantly bracket a realistic budget estimate for each line item. This allows you to become proactive in your spending habits as well as plan for future expenditures. For example, there are periodic larger expenses such as tuition, insurance premiums, etc that can be programmed months ahead of time. In other words, you could overstate a line items budget with the idea of saving for the periodic larger expense. Or, you could just put the planned excess into the savings portion of the disposable income section.

 Personal Financial Statement

When the loan officer reviews the personal financial statement they are looking mainly at the following considerations:

- Net Worth: How much in unencumbered (free of debt obligations) assets can be used as security (if needed) to cover the loan amount?
- Free Cash Flow: Given the regular income and expenses reported, how would the contemplated loan payment amount affect the borrower's ability to meet existing financial obligations?

As we will see in the Chapter on Credit, besides looking at the Personal Financial Statement, loan officers also normally check employment, credit scores and often times personal references.

The recent financial crisis was caused mainly because many lenders relaxed their normal credit worthiness due diligence processes. The federal government through its Government Sponsored Entities (GSE) of Fanny Mae and Freddie Mac, actually put pressure on lenders to loosen up credit checks to allow for more home loans in an effort to pump up the economy. As a result, too many loans were made to borrowers who really couldn't afford the loans. As soon as these "sub-prime" loans started to default, housing prices dropped and it started an avalanche of risky home loan defaults which almost brought down the entire credit industry. As a result, applying for credit will return to perhaps even more rigorous qualification procedures.

Below is a personal financial statement.

ASSETS (Omit Cents)	LIABILITIES (Omit Cents)
Cash on hand & in Banks ....$ _____	Accounts Payable.............................$ _____
Savings Accounts ....$ _____	Notes Payable to Banks and Others ....$ _____
IRA or Other Retirement Account........$ _____	(Describe in Section 2)
Accounts & Notes Receivable ....$ _____	Installment Account (Auto) ....$ _____
Life Insurance-Cash Surrender Value Only....... $ ....(Complete Section B)	Mo. Payments $ _____
	Installment Account (Other)................$ _____
	Mo. Payments $ _____
Stocks and Bonds............................$ _____ (Describe in Section 3)	Loan on Life Insurance ....$ _____
Real Estate ....$ _____ (Describe in Section 4)	Mortgages on Real Estate.................$ _____ (Describe in Section 4)
Automobile-Present Value................$ _____	Unpaid Taxes ....$ _____ (Describe in Section 6)
Other Personal Property..................$ _____ (Describe in Section 5)	Other Liabilities................................$ _____ (Describe in Section 7)
Other Assets...................................$ _____ (Describe in Section 5)	Total Liabilities................................ $ Net Worth .... $
Total $	Total $
Section 1. Source of Income	**Contingent Liabilities**
Salary .... $ Net Investment Income............................ $ Real Estate Income .... $ Other Income (Describe below)* .... $	As Endorser or Co-Maker................................. $ Legal Claims & Judgments........................ $ Provision for Federal Income Tax.............. $ Other Special Debt .... $

 Cash Flow Management: Where Did the Money Go?

A budget looks so nice and neat on paper, but unfortunately expenses and the available cash to pay for them do not always coincide. Because of this fact, many people suffer the stress of periods of being "broke." Of course, sometimes things happen. But that's one of the reasons for always having some emergency funds immediately available. However, part of keeping a financial house in order requires some cash flow management.

Perhaps the best way to illustrate cash flow management is to use an example that relates to a typical university student.

Example Cash Flow Expense Calendar

Day	Income	Expense	Balance	Day	Income	Expense	Balance
1	$900		$900	16		Clothing $100	850
2		Rent $475	425	17		Cash $50	800
3		Food $100	325	18		0	
4		0		19		0	
5		0		20		Food $100	700
6		Cash $50	275	21		Books $75	625
7		0		22		Cash $50	575
8		0		23		0	
9		Laundry $10	265	24		0	
10		Utilities, Phone $65	200	25		Health Club $110	465
11		Food $100	100	26		Credit Card $200	265
12		Cash $50	50	27		Food $100	165
13		0		28		Cash $50	115
14		0		29		0	
15	$900		950	30		Cash $50	65
	Danger Zone						

As you can see, there are points in the month where any hiccup like not getting the check from home can become a time when a close eye must be kept on expenditures. If you make the effort to do a budget, which is highly recommended, you should also do a cash flow calendar. Both help you to become aware of what you have to work with and when it might be time to become concerned. It allows for better planning and less stressful moments. Indeed, you want to become an expert on the care and feeding of yourself. Besides, as you start the climb up the income ladder, the number of your transactions increase and it becomes more difficult to know exactly where you stand in terms of future cash needs. Again, most people use their checkbook balance as an indicator of financial position but this is a reactive strategy rather than proactive financial management. Besides, how many people actually keep their checkbook balance up-to-date?

A budget and cash flow planning go hand-in-hand. It's not so much about becoming an overly conservative pencil pusher as it is more about becoming a responsible and prepared person living in a complex society. The earlier you get into the habits of good financial management, the better it will serve you throughout your life. Indeed, not applying these simple procedures usually has a good sized price tag.

 Economic Terminology

These common terms can help act as signposts and warning signs for employers, consumers and workers. While it is tacitly agreed that statistics can be manipulated and misleading, that doesn't mean that they should be discarded out of hand. Indeed, most public policy is based upon the information being served up to the public. As one gets older and more experienced, it can become great sport reading between the lines of what is said and what is actually meant. In fact, many of the common economic terms are today's version of reading tea leaves or the entrails read by the ancient mystics trying to decipher the whimsies of the capricious gods who liked toying with the lives of men and women. Some might say that the analogy is more than just metaphorical.

Economic Terminology you should become familiar with:

Gross Domestic Product (GDP): This is the "big picture" data point that demonstrates the general comparative level of production of the U.S. economy. More specifically, it measures the value of all goods and services produced in the United States during a calendar year- minus exports, government spending and products made by U.S. companies in foreign markets.

For the mature developed economies of the U.S., most European countries and Japan, an annual percentage in the range of 2% to 4% GDP growth is considered as healthy.

Indeed, a percentage increase greater than 4% usually means that the economy may be overheating and measures might be taken to slow down the economy. By the same token, a GDP moving below 2% may demonstrate a weak economy and would call for stimulative measures to help boost output. As a general anecdote, when GDP declines for two consecutive quarters, many economists consider the economy to be in recession.

Consumer Confidence Index: As the U.S. economy derives over 70% of GDP from the consumption of goods and services, it is important to keep track of how willing consumers are to purchase. Logically, the more confident they feel, the more likely that the economy will benefit. This index gives a good sense of how Americans feel about the current economic environment and about their future expectations. The index is published monthly by the Consumer Research Center of the Conference Board and is based on a representative sample of 5,000 U.S. households.

Employment Cost Index: This index is used to monitor inflation by measuring changes in labor costs for money wages and salaries. It also measures non-cash fringe benefits in non-farm private industry and in state and local government. It is provided quarterly by the Bureau of Labor Statistics. If labor related costs are going up, that will mean that those costs will most likely be passed on to consumers, which can mean price increases. An increase in the ECI might imply that steps might be taken to reduce inflation-usually by raising interest rates to dampen economic growth.

Index of Leading Economic Indicators (LEI or ILEI): This index consists of eleven economic reports, such as initial unemployment claims, stock-market activity, building permits, new orders for consumer goods, plant and equipment orders and sensitive material prices. As the name implies, the LEI is an attempt to get an idea of where the future (six months out) might be heading. In fact, three consecutive increases in the LEI may suggest that the economy has begun to increase activity.

Industrial Production: The U.S. Federal Reserve offers a monthly informed view on the status of key industries in the U.S. economy. Specifically, it shows the change in output for three sectors: manufacturing, mining, and the gas- and electric-utility industries. Some argue that as the U.S. is evolving more into a provider of services such as financial and technical consulting and software that this index may need to be modified to reflect the changing nature of the U.S. economy.

Consumer Price Index (CPI): As mentioned before, this index is supposed to tell you whether prices are rising or falling. It's published each month by the Bureau of Labor Statistics. The CPI tracks the price changes for a fixed basket of goods and services, from bread and milk to cars and energy. CPI or Customer Price Index measures how price changes over time for different areas of expenses. For example, the CPI might be tracked for transportation or medical care.

Inflation: The cost of having a modern economy and, like a chronic illness, it can be managed. The Federal Reserve Banking system is charged with the double edged responsibility of creating jobs while at the same time controlling inflation; a juggling act that affects hundreds of millions not only in the U.S. but with implications for the global world. However, keep in mind that the modern economy is based largely on perception and he who controls the information can control the perception.

Unemployment Rate and First-Time Jobless Claims: The unemployment rate is the percentage of American workers who are out of work. "First-time jobless claims" is the number of people filing for unemployment benefits for the first time. These important indicators are provided by the Department of Labor on a weekly basis. As with many of these statistics, there are some concerns for what they don't say. For example, the BLS calculates the official unemployment rate, U-3, as the number of unemployed as a percentage of the civilian labor force. The civilian labor force consists of employed workers plus the officially unemployed, those without jobs who are available to work and have looked for a job in the last four weeks. The comprehensive U-6 unemployment rate adjusts the official rate by adding marginally attached workers and workers forced to work part time for economic reasons to the officially unemployed. To find the U-6 rate, the BLS takes that higher unemployment count and divides it by the official civilian labor force plus the number of marginally attached workers. (No adjustment is necessary for forced part-time workers since they are already counted in the official labor force as employed workers.) If one uses the combined U-3 and U-6, unemployment rate is actually much higher than the customarily reported U-3 index. So, which one would you prefer to publicize? Again, we see that "truth" can be a relative thing.

Fed funds rate or Discount Rate: Every month, the Federal Open Market Committee (FOMC) meets to decide what changes, if any, should be made in this fundamental economic tool to control the direction of the economy. The Fed funds rate is the interest rate the central bank charges member banks for borrow overnight funds. All other interest rates in the economy are influenced by this rate. If the rate goes up, that usually means that the economy may be overheating and needs to be slowed down. On the other hand, if the rate is lowered, that may mean that the economy is sluggish and may need lower cost of borrowing to help stimulate the economy.

This short list of economic terms presents some of the most commonly used for public consumption. These numbers are put out there to help the common citizen have a picture of what is happening but as usual, statistics can be misleading. For example, a 7% unemployment rate may indicate a slowing economy. The full effect of such a number can be abstract or stark reality. Indeed, as the old saying goes, "When your neighbor is out of work, it's called a recession. When you are out of work, it's a depression."

 Sample Test Questions - Chapter 1

1) People accept the local currency in a financial transaction because it

   A) Is printed by the state government
   B) Is customary to do so
   C) Is tacitly agreed to that the currency has a certain value
   D) Is printed by the Federal Reserve System

The correct answer is C:) It is tacitly agreed to that the currency has a certain value. When a government loses credibility either from excessive inflation or other political-economic problems, people will look for better ways to protect their wealth. For example, if the prices are in hyperinflation and rising 10% each day, money received today would be worth half as much in just five days.

2) The U.S. dollar is backed by

   A) Gold
   B) Silver
   C) Custom
   D) Full faith and credit of the U.S. Treasury

The correct answer is D:) Full faith and credit of the U.S. Treasury. In other words, the dollar is based upon faith in the U.S. Treasury to be responsible. When that faith disappears, so does the value in the dollar.

3) Typically, inflation is the result of

   A) Too few dollars in circulation
   B) An oversupply of money and an increasing propensity for consumption
   C) An increase in interest rates
   D) Lower unemployment rates

The correct answer is B:) An oversupply of money and an increasing propensity for consumption. Prices will usually be pushed up when there is too many dollars chasing too few goods. The increased demand puts pressure on resources such as raw materials and labor. This can cause those factors of production to increase and then be passed on to the consumer in the form of higher prices. However, the recent China import revolution has allowed the costs of production to be shifted to a low wage economy and this has helped to keep down price inflation in the importing nations.

4) The CPI measures

   A) The cost producer index
   B) The rate of inflation in raw materials
   C) The consumer price index
   D) The price of a basket of over 80,000 different consumer items and compares the rate of increase or decrease in the cost of the hypothetical basket

The correct answer is D:) The price of a basket of over 80,000 different consumer items and compares the rate of increase or decrease in the cost of the hypothetical basket. Many economists feel that the basket misses some important items such as housing prices, the cost of crude oil and other important or volatile items.

5) What is one of the main reasons banks and other financial institutions pay interest to depositors?

   A) To compete with other lending institutions
   B) To compensate depositors for the effects of inflation
   C) To provide depositors a way to preserve wealth
   D) To be able to pay salaries to employees

The correct answer is B:) To compensate depositors for the effects of inflation. There are bank accounts such as checking accounts that normally don't pay interest. Money that is kept in reserve in savings accounts will lose value over time due to the effects of inflation. Even though paying depositors interest does help preserve some protection against inflation, most interest rates paid to depositors are below the inflation rate and does not totally preserve the value of monies on deposit.

6) Learning how to establish a budget provides a process to

   A) Match income with expenses.
   B) Become conscious of consumption patterns.
   C) Plan consumption and not to exceed income. Budgeting also provides a disciplined way to save income.
   D) Not exceed income in any given time period.

The correct answer is C:) Plan consumption and not to exceed income. Budgeting also provides a disciplined way to save income. It also helps to achieve financial goals once they are defined.

7) What is meant by "expenses rise to meet income"?

   A) If your expenses go up, so will your income
   B) If you start making more money, your expenses will rise
   C) If your income rises, you will have a tendency to spend more
   D) If your income rises, you should keep a close watch on your expenses

The correct answer is C:) If your income rises, you will have a tendency to spend more. There is a well known economic phenomenon called "the wealth effect." It states that as a person feels wealthier, they will improve their lifestyle. Unfortunately, the wealth effect has a downside because when people lose wealth, they prefer to keep their lifestyle and this can lead to bankruptcy.

8) One of the best ways to use budgeting to help create wealth is?

   A) Add "savings" as an expense line item
   B) Reduce all expenses by 10%
   C) Write a check to savings from the disposable income before paying bills
   D) Write a check to savings after paying all the bills

The correct answer is C:) Write a check to savings from the disposable income before paying bills. If you know what your income is and what your spending will be, you can figure out the disposable income (income less expenses) and write a check to savings for certain percentage of the estimated disposable income and then make yourself stick closely to the budget. Savings should be taken out of estimated disposable income before the month otherwise there will be a tendency to let expenses "creep" and cut into the disposable income portion of the budget.

9) It is important to do an annual personal business plan because it

   A) Makes you take time and give some thought to what your personal and financial goals are
   B) Forces you to sit down and write out what you want to achieve in the way of personal and financial goals. The plan also helps formulate strategies on how to achieve those goals.
   C) A plan acts as a wish list
   D) When you actually are making good money, you will need to do some planning

The correct answer is B:) Forces you to sit down and write out what you want to achieve in the way of personal, professional and financial goals. The plan also helps formulate strategies on how to achieve those goals.

10) When seeking credit and asked to fill out a personal financial statement, the lender wants to see that

   A) You are working at a steady job
   B) The lender can secure the loan with some of your assets
   C) You have paid your bills
   D) You have more assets than liabilities and that a new payment amount will fit within your capabilities to pay on a regular basis

The correct answer is D:) You have more assets than liabilities and that a new payment amount will fit within your capabilities to pay on a regular basis. Of course, there are other factors, but this is perhaps the most critical.

11) When you set up a budget, it is also a good idea to produce a _____ to make sure you don't run out of money during the month.

   A) Financial statement
   B) Personal business plan
   C) Non disclosure statement
   D) Cash flow forecast calendar

The correct answer is D:) Cash flow forecast calendar. Just having a budget doesn't mean that you might not run out of cash due to the timing of income and expenses.

12) When reporting the unemployment rate, the number used by the government usually _____ the number of unemployed.

   A) Understates
   B) Overstates
   C) Uses the U-3 formula
   D) Uses the U-6 formula

The correct answer is C:) Uses the U-3 formula. This formula includes the number of unemployed as a percentage of the civilian labor force. The civilian labor force consists of employed workers plus the officially unemployed, those without jobs who are available to work and have looked for a job in the last 4 weeks. Many people feel that the rate should use both the U-3 and U-6 formulas which would produce a significantly higher rate of unemployment.

13) The Fed funds rate is the interest rate that the_____ charges member banks for overnight loans.

   A) Treasury Department
   B) New York Fed
   C) FOMC
   D) Central Bank

The correct answer is D:) Central Bank. The FOMC is a committee which decides on if there are to be any changes in the Fed funds rate.

14) If you hear that the unemployment rate is starting to creep up, you might expect that the _____might _____ the Fed funds rate.

   A) Central Bank, decrease
   B) FOMC, increase
   C) Central Bank, increase
   D) FOMC, decrease

The correct answer is D:) FOMC, decrease. If it looks as if the economy is slowing down, the FOMC might want to lower the Fed funds rate to help stimulate the economy and more employment.

15) You are trying to buy a home and you fill out a personal financial statement. You have a car that's worth about $11,000, a bank account with $2,500, a computer worth 1,000. You have a credit card balance of 10,000, which requires a minimum payment of $250 per month and a student loan balance of $ 5,000 and a monthly payment of $450 per month. Your Net Worth is _____.

   A) $4,500
   B) $13,800
   C) -$500
   D) -$1,200

The correct answer is C:) -$500. Assets-liabilities=net worth. Although cash flow is important in determining the ability to pay for a new loan, unsecured, callable loans are usually concerned as potentially due at any time and thus the total liabilities must be used and not just the payment.

Chapter 2 - Credit and Debit

If there has been one financial factor that has allowed for the rapid growth and improvement in standards of living in the U.S., it is the use of credit. It provides for a massive increase in the velocity of money and number of transactions. In fact, credit allows a consumer, business or government to acquire assets today and pay for them tomorrow, usually with devalued money. Let's take an example of the American Dream: owning your own home to demonstrate the importance of credit.

Housing is a necessity and most people either rent or own. To own a home or apartment in the U.S. has become an expensive proposition for most and without access to credit, being able to purchase a home would be a near impossibility. Only the wealthy would own property and the rest of us would be tenants with no vested interest in the property. Indeed, in the early history of the U.S., you needed to be a property owner to be able to vote and that was quickly determined not to be very compatible in a democracy. Today, purchasing a home is still a symbol of becoming a vested member in society and a symbolic gesture of becoming a full-fledged member of the property owning middle class. Not only that, construction is a huge industry and employs either directly or indirectly millions of Americans (and illegal aliens). Indeed, the jobs provided by new construction help to generate the very purchasing power needed to buy a home. But, without credit, the American Dream would be just that-a dream beyond the financial reach of most people to realize.

The median household income in the U.S. is about $49,000 gross (before taxes). After taxes, that translates into about $3200 per month. The median price for a home in a metropolitan area such as Minneapolis is about $184,000 (third quarter 2009). Without credit, how would the average American worker purchase a home-particularly given that the U.S. savings rate is about 3% of income?

Using that savings rate, a median income family saving 3% of $3200 per month would save about $96 per month or about $1152 per year. At that rate, it would take over 100 years to save enough to purchase a home in Minneapolis at a price set a century in the past. In other words it's not going to happen. So, given the importance of owning a home in a free, capitalistic society, the development of the property mortgage made owning a home a feasible proposition. In fact, up until about the late 1960s, most individuals usually just needed credit for the purpose of purchasing a home. Credit cards and even most car loans didn't become common and easily available until the late 1960s and early 1970s.

Here is the basic thinking behind the parameters for lending money for the purchase of a home.

1. As the home is used as security for the loan itself, the value of the security will most probably increase in value over time and at least help compensate for the long range rate of inflation.

2. A credit worthy borrower will continue at the same or better income level over the life of the loan.

3. As the home will acts as security for the loan, if the loan goes into default, there will be a ready market to help liquidate the property and recapture the balance of the loan.

4. The borrower will pay for property damage insurance and in many cases life insurance to pay off the loan (a loan to purchase secured property is called a mortgage) incase the main breadwinner(s) dies.

5. The borrower will pay principle and sufficient interest to cover inflation and provide additional income to the lender for taking the risk.

6. The borrower will exercise pride of ownership and properly maintain the property.

However, to make sure that the borrower has some vested interest in the property, a down payment is usually required by the lender and the balance of the sales price be collateralized over a long period of time, usually 30 years. Typically, a borrower has to have at least 10-20% of the total sales price to qualify for the loan along with going through a thorough credit investigation looking for past credit payment history. Generally, a person must have a 20% down payment to avoid paying for Private Mortgage Insurance (PMI). So, once a borrower has been qualified, they can take out a loan which usually costs less than paying rent for similar housing. The lender gets a "secured" steady return on the loan and the borrower gets the right to build up equity in the home. An interest only mortgage is a mortgage for which the minimum monthly payment only covers interest. In a reverse mortgage, a person receives payments based on the equity of their house instead of making payments to own it.

Equity is the difference between the sale price and the outstanding loan at the time of the sale. Equity builds when the value of the home increases and as the loan gets paid down. Indeed, it's a win-win-win: a win for the borrower, who now owns a home, a win for the lender because they make passive income (not having to produce any work for the revenue) secured by a tangible asset and a win for the economy as the construction industry reduces available inventory and makes way for new construction, which creates many related jobs.

As long as the majority of the loans (mortgages) are not affected by any adverse changes, credit provides a lot of positive factors to society. However, as has happened with the current credit crisis, sometimes, ambitious and greedy players play the system. One of the main reasons for the recent financial crisis is the lack of proper qualification of home buyers which made it easy for buyers to qualify with no equity to keep them from walking away from the loan. Not only that, the normal procedures for qualifying borrowers was side stepped by most of the lending industry. It was all about gaining market share and little about risk taking. The result was an avalanche of mortgage defaults which left many lenders with no revenue from the loans they made as well as an asset with declining value as abandoned homes flooded the market.

Of course, there were other factors, but the most severe credit crisis since the great depression was brought on by abuse of the normal process of mortgage lending. Naturally, when housing and construction hit a pot hole, many hundreds of thousands of construction related jobs were lost dragging the entire economy down as lenders tried to put a hold on most credit until there was adequate funding again and proper credit procedures were put back into place.

Having access to credit is also very important for businesses that need credit to meet the cash flow swings suffered by most companies. The reality of credit is that many companies don't get paid for their products or services in rhythm with their expense cycles. For example, many businesses have payroll due on the 15th and last day of the month yet they may not get paid for products and services for 60 or more days. To help "float" the payroll, companies need credit.

Businesses also need credit to expand opportunities and help create more profits for the company and more jobs for the economy. Indeed, many governments need to finance much of their operating budgets because of shortfalls in tax revenues. Unfortunately, the U.S. government has become the world's largest debtor nation having to borrow trillions of dollars each year to "stay in business." Governments can do that because they can just print more money as long as it doesn't cause too many concerns about inflation and a country's ability to function and produce over the long run.

 # Secured and Unsecured Credit

Most loans are classified by two main types of credit: secured and unsecured.

Secured Credit: The main risk to lenders is default by the borrowers. Often times conditions change and a borrower who once looked solid suffers a set-back like losing a job or becoming incapacitated. In which case, a lender would like to have some recourse in order to recover some or the entire loan made to the borrower. One of the best ways to make a loan and help reduce the risk of losing all or a large part of a loan is by having pre-established rights to a tangible asset that has an estimated market value in excess of the loan. Banks make home loans and have the right to the title of the property if certain loan requirements aren't met. Car loans are the same; the lender has rights to the title of the car if a loan is in default. Typically, the more the risk, the more the collateral required to secure the loan. Moreover, the more risk, the higher the interest rate. For instance, a home loan may charge 6% interest while an car loan might charge a 12% interest rate. It's a lot easier to steal or run off with an car than a home.

Unsecured Credit: An unsecured loan is a risky loan in that the lender has no rights to the property purchased with the credit. Credit cards are the prime example and the only counter balance to the high risk is to charge a high rate of interest, threaten a borrower's credit score or take legal action in a civil court.

Many people complain about the high interest charged by credit cards-sometimes in excess of 25%. But consider that the amount of unreimbursed credit card loans can reach up to over 13% of the total lending. In an effort to cover these loses, credit card companies charge high rates and spread the risk across the population of credit card holders and to make a return on their investment.

Other common types of unsecured loans are student loans, some credit lines, retail company credit cards and the most common-vendor terms. Vendor terms refer to the ability of a business to purchase goods and services from another business with a promise to pay within a certain specified time period-usually 30 days. These promises to pay are called accounts payable for the borrower and accounts receivable for the lender of credit. Indeed, this type of credit is essential for smoothly functioning markets.

Unsecured loans are risky yet have become an essential part of an American consumer society based upon impulse buying and instant gratification. When a consumer sees an item they want, all they need to do is pull out a credit card and bingo, whether or not they have the money, they can purchase the product or service. This facility drives the volume of transactions and greases the flow of commerce. Before the era of easy credit, consumers needed to plan way ahead for the purchase of a good or service and only make the transaction when they had the money to pay for it. This is called deferred gratification. But that meant fewer sales not only because consumers might change their minds over time but also it reduces the opportunities for idle funds to earn passive income by being lent out.

Credit Cards

Credit cards can be like matches in the hands of a young child if not handled with responsibility. As most credit cards charge no interest if paid in full within 30 days, it's OK to use a credit card if you will be paying it off within the 30 day billing cycle. In this way, a credit card can provide not only a record of each purchase but also help smooth out any cash flow problems. But, if you can't pay the balance off within the 30 day billing cycle, you should not use a credit card unless it's an emergency. Credit cards can be very useful but they must be used with caution and discipline. The credit companies want you to overspend your budget so you will have to start paying those high interest rates and they make a lot of money because most people lack the discipline to pay off balances quickly. Indeed, the more we "press plastic," the easier it is to overspend and wind up paying interest.

Is it a good idea to get a credit card?
The answer is yes. It allows you to build up a positive credit record, provides emergency funds and allows close tracking of expenditures, but only if you pay off the balance within the 30 day interest free grace period. However, if you can't control your consumption impulses, stay away from credit cards.

It's even more important to establish a budget if you are planning to use a credit or debit card. If you know your financial parameters, you can act with discipline. Without a budget, a credit card will most likely take you down the road to unnecessary stress and a dubious credit record.

Interest Rates

An interest rate is the yearly price that a lender will charge you for borrowing their money. So, if you borrow $10,000 at a 7% simple interest rate for one year, the money earned on the loan would be $700 per year. Let's say over the life of a three year loan you paid $3,000 in interest and you had borrowed $10,000 for three years. What would be the interest rate you paid?

To find out the APR (annual percentage rate) you can use this formula:
(Interest paid ÷ Loan amount) x 100 ÷ number of years
In our example: ($3,000 ÷ $10,000) x 100 ÷ 3 years = 30% ÷ 3 = 10% interest per year.

Keep this formula in mind because there are many types of interest and the actual interest paid may differ from that advertised. So, when you are thinking about getting a loan, take the total amount paid in interest and charges and divide by the loan amount to find out the real interest to be paid.

Types of Interest

Nominal interest is the stated interest rate. It is the number used in the formula for determining the interest to be paid.

Real interest is the nominal interest rate minus the inflation rate. For example, one year bonds pay about 1% but the official inflation rate is about 2.5% so there is a real interest rate of -1.5% meaning a loss of 1.5% in purchasing power over the year. So why would an investor buy a one year bond? Answer: safety of the principal.

Simple interest is calculated only on the principal amount that you borrowed originally, or on that portion of the principal amount which remains unpaid.

Compound Interest is similar to simple interest. However, over time, the difference between the amount of interest paid can be considerably larger when compared to simple interest. This difference is because unpaid interest is added to the balance due.

For example: Loan terms: $10,000 for 10 years @ 7%

Simple interest: would be $700 per year or $58.33 per month in interest.

Compound interest: ($10,000 loan + $7,000 interest to be charged over the life of the loan)= $17, 000 x 7% = $1190 per year or $99 per month in interest.

How Interest Rates Are Determined

Loan interest rates, commonly called the cost of money, are concerned with two major concepts:

- Hedging inflation (preserving the value of money over time)
- Compensation for risk

When governments, companies and individuals have funds not being used for operational or living expenses, the desire is to "park" the funds in an investment vehicle that can produce passive income. A chain of events happen before market makers and lenders can build up a case for a specific cost for borrowing money. The first step starts with the Federal Open Market Committee (FOMC) which is a branch of the Federal Reserve Bank. Each month, the FOMC meets to decide what the federal funds discount rate should be. This interest rate is the amount of interest that the central bank will charge member banks for borrowing short term money (overnight funds). From this interest rate, banks and other lenders can begin to build a series of charges for loans based upon a "spread" between the wholesale cost of money and what it can generate in profits for what it can be lent for. For example, if a bank can borrow money from the central bank for 1%, it can then begin to build a revenue model of how the lender will cover all operational expenses and make a profit while at the same time keeping risk in the form of loan defaults to a minimum. To do that, once the costs of making a loan are developed, a more subjective process of analyzing how much of the interest rate to be charged will pay for the risk level of the loan.

Institutional Loan Evaluation and Interest Rate Fixing Process Flow

Each loan application is analyzed and usually ends up in the Loan Committee where a final decision is rendered. Of course, loans can be constructed in many ways to help reduce risk to the lender. For example, a lender is more willing to take risks if the borrower provides sufficient security, more equity in the form of a larger down payment, a reduction in the length of the loan or provides a credit worthy co-signatory on the loan. Indeed, finance and credit can be incredibly creative and complex. The business of lending funds attempts to devise a transaction that meets the needs of both lender and borrower and that quantitative meeting point is reflected in the terms and interest rate.

Credit Scores and Credit Reporting

When you apply for credit, usually for a credit card, a car loan, or a mortgage, lenders want to know what risk they'd take by loaning money to you. FICO scores (named after the software developed by Fair Isaac and Company) are the credit scores most lenders use to determine your credit risk. You have three FICO scores, one for each of the three credit bureaus: Experian, TransUnion, and Equifax. Each score is based on information all or some of the credit bureau's information about your finances. As this information changes, your credit scores tend to change as well. If you are late on payments or default on any loans, the events are recorded and affect you FICO scores. It is the exceptions to good consumer behavior they want to know about. Don't expect accolades for paying on time. It's the one you forget that they want to know about. It is important to understand that once impaired, credit scores can be improved and taking steps to monitor, protect and improve your FICO scores can help you qualify for better rates from lenders. A good credit rating can save you money.

Lenders depend heavily on FICO scores to asses risk based on a consumer's payment history; the higher the score, the better. However, not only lenders turn to credit scores for some indication of with whom they are dealing. In many circumstances, having a decent credit score can be part of the due diligence in screening potential tenants, business associates, candidates for employment and any other process for investigating a person's level of financial credibility and behavior. While some feel credit scores are intrusive, they are becoming more important in our daily lives. Indeed, it's no longer the family name or other anecdotal information that lends credence to who you might be. For many situations, your credit score is who you are.

 FICO Scores

Having a higher FICO score makes a difference in the level of interest charged. The higher your score, the better your credit. It may not seem like much but it translates into APR (annual percentage rate) as a 25% discount for having the highest score (760-850) as compared to the lowest (620-639).

FICO scores have different names at each of the credit reporting agencies. All of these scores, however, are developed using the same methods by Fair Isaac software. Although most lenders rely on the FICO scores as part of their loan process, several factors need to be understood:

- The three major credit bureaus are not the only scores used. Some lenders use their own credit sources as well as FICO
- Credit scores can be different for each credit bureau. Each bureau evaluates credit history in different ways
- FICO scores constantly change over time

Seven Year Records

If you are late paying bills or default on any debts, those black marks will stay on your credit report for seven years before they can be expunged from your record. In a consumer society, having access to credit is an important part of taking advantage of the good things a modern economic system has to offer. However, it's essential that you pay all your bills on time, all the time. Set up automatic payments or a reminder systems so that you're never, ever late. All it takes is a single missed payment to trash your credit scores – and it can take seven years for the effects to completely disappear.

To get good credit and keep it, you should do the following:

- Check your credit report. Each year, you are entitled to a free credit report which will allow you to see if there are any errors (which often happen). Contact Equifax, Experian or Trans Union directly.
- Have checking and savings accounts in good standing
- Have someone else add you to their credit, by piggybacking. The fastest way to establish a credit history is to "borrow" someone else's record, either by being added to a credit card as a joint account holder or by getting someone to co-sign a loan for you.

For example, if your father has good credit and adds you to his credit card, his history with that account can be imported to your credit bureau file, giving you an instant credit record.

- Apply for credit while you're a college student
- Apply for a secured credit or debit card. If you can't get a regular credit card, apply for the secured version. These require you to deposit money with a lender; your credit limit is usually equal to the deposit. These typically charge very high interest so only use as a last resort.
- Observe the following with all credit cards:
  - Don't charge more than 30% of the card's limit
  - Don't charge more than you can pay off in a month
  - Make sure you pay the bill, and all your other bills, on time

Many students take out loans to help finance their educations. Always pay these loans on time. Once you get your first job after graduation, it is easy to forget student loans but the liability doesn't stop after you graduate. In fact, it is an excellent idea to place student loans as your highest priority debt or if you have multiple debts, pay off the one with the highest interest rate first.

Credit Repair

If for some unfortunate reason you damage your credit rating, there is an entire industry ready to help you get back into a healthier credit worthy state. These credit repair counselors help you establish the discipline to needed to improve your credit score. Can they help bypass the seven year limitations on expungement of your credit record? The answer is no, but they can demonstrate to a lender that you have seen the light and have taken a proactive approach to avoid any such events from happening again.

Bankruptcy

Even people with a long record of good credit can suffer the misfortunes of risk. However, the recent growth in personal bankruptcy has been alarming. The concept of bankruptcy was originally set up to help companies preserve jobs and arrange for new debt restructuring. However, over the recent years the intent of saving companies has made a subtle migration to saving individual consumers. Perhaps it was brought about by bankruptcy lawyers developing new opportunities but many undisciplined consumers used personal bankruptcy laws to play the system. In an effort to change this escape of personal responsibility, the Congress passed the Bankruptcy Abuse Prevention and Consumer Protection Act in October, 2005.

Bankruptcy is the most drastic legal remedy for dealing with unpaid debts you can't pay. There are two major types of bankruptcy in regards to consumers: Chapter 13 and Chapter 7.

Under **Chapter 13,** a plan to pay back some or all of the debt is arranged between debtor and creditors with the assistance and guidance of a third party-the civil courts. Under **Chapter 7**, there are no attempts to payback debt owed. Instead, any assets owned by the debtor are liquidated for payment to the creditors and all other debts discharged.

Chapter 11 bankruptcy is also called reorganization. This primarily used in businesses and allows the owner to remain in charge and work out a manageable payment plan.

Chapter 20 bankruptcy does not actually exist. It receives that name because it occurs by first filing for Chapter 7 bankruptcy, and then Chapter 13 bankruptcy. This way the debtor can relieve themselves of as much debt as possible, and then work out a plan to pay off the rest of their debt.

In the recent past, the professionally unscrupulous turned to easy credit to finance fraudulent activities. By the time fraud was detected, assets had been moved offshore and protected from liquidation and creditors were left with no recourse. However, the call of easy credit also found too many undisciplined borrowers overextended and unable to pay debt. Combined with an unstable economy and job layoffs, millions of overextended workers found themselves unable to pay back their debts. Before October 17, 2005 it was relatively painless to file for Chapter 13 bankruptcy and walk away from financial obligations while preserving substantial personal assets. Bankruptcy has its downside as it will stay on your credit report for up to ten years.

Too Much Credit

Banks saw the need to compensate for the low rates of interest they could charge on loans so they developed a strategy of blanketing the consumer with easy unsecured debt. The idea was that there would be an acceptable number of defaults that would be more than compensated for by the high rates being charged to the entire set of credit card holders.

The danger is that money may become so abstract that it loses its value. By exercising planning and discipline, we can demonstrate its worth. Because credit can be a valuable tool in development and the creation of jobs, governments, companies and individuals must apply the responsible ways of handling money. Bankruptcy is the public acknowledgement of bad luck, ineptness or irresponsible money management. Much too often, bankruptcy is the end game for fraudulent business models.

 *Sample Test Questions - Chapter 2*

1) To home mortgage lenders, one of the worst things that can happen is

   A) The home owner dies
   B) The home owner loses their job
   C) The property declines in value
   D) The competition offers lower interest rates

The correct answer is C:) The property declines in value. Having the ability to sell the home and recuperate the loan in case of a default depends on a ready market and sustainable asset value. Declining home values was a major factor in fomenting the recent financial crisis of 2008. This happened because lending institutions are highly leveraged and a slight decline in the value of their assets can have a large effect on their ability to stay operational. Normally, a bank is only required to have about 8% of its assets in liquid form. Once below that level of required capital, a bank can no longer make loans. As a result, a sinking housing market like the one in mid 2008 forced many banks to suspend operations because of the violation of the minimum capital requirements. This in turn made it very difficult for businesses and individuals to have access to much needed credit. Once the layoffs began, it started to bring down the entire economy.

2) Which of the following would most likely have the lowest interest rate?

   A) Loan for an car
   B) Loan for a home
   C) Personal loan secured by tangible property
   D) Credit card

The correct answer is B:) Loan for a home. This is because real estate is easier to value, re-sell and is usually in high demand.

3) The most important interest rate to the economy in general is the

   A) Federal funds rate
   B) Home mortgage rates
   C) Credit card rates
   D) The ten year U.S. Treasury bill

The correct answer is A:) Federal funds rate. This is the rate that the central bank charges member banks to borrow short term funds. This federal funds rate is the first in a series of rates that go into the construction of various costs for borrowing money.

4) The _____ sets the federal funds rate.

   A) Central Bank of New York
   B) U.S. Treasury
   C) Federal Reserve Chairman
   D) FOMC

The correct answer is D:) FOMC. The Federal Open Market Committee reviews and establishes the federal funds rate. The committee meets monthly to review the current economic situation and decide if there should be any changes to the rate and/or other ways to help promote economic growth while at the same time control inflation.

5) Interests rates are mainly concerned with these two factors: _____ and _____.

   A) Capital preservation, inflation
   B) Compensation for risk, the Fed funds rate
   C) Preservation of the value of funds against inflation, compensation for risk
   D) Profitability, liquidity of funds

The correct answer is C:) Preservation of the value of funds against inflation, compensation for risk.

6) If a bank borrows money from the central bank for 1% and then loans it out at 7%, what would be the bank's "spread"? The bank needs at least 3% of a loan for operational costs.

   A) 6%
   B) 3%
   C) 4%
   D) 7%

The correct answer is A:) 6%. A spread is not the profit margin. It is the difference between two rates.

7) The three major credit bureaus are: _____, _____ and _____.

   A) Equifax, Trans Union and First Federal
   B) Experian, Equifax and Trans Union
   C) Trans Central, Esperian and Exxon
   D) FOMC, First Federal, First Union

The correct answer is B:) Experian, Equifax and Trans Union.

8) Each credit bureau report provides _____ on the _____ information provided.

   A) The same scores, same information
   B) Different scores, same information
   C) Different scores, different information
   D) The same scores, different information

The correct answer is B:) Different scores, same information. This is because each bureau uses a slightly different formula placing different weights on different factors. That's why most lending agencies require more than one bureau score.

9) If you had a FICO score of _____ you would be considered in the top grouping.

   A) 800+
   B) 650+
   C) 400+
   D) 200+

The answer is A:) 800+. Only about 13% of the credit applicants are in this group.

10) If you wanted to find out your credit score, you most probably would

   A) Contact your state consumer agency
   B) Apply for credit and pay a fee for a report
   C) Contact one of the bureaus once per year and ask for your obligatory free report
   D) Ask your bank to provide you with your most recent credit score

The correct answer is C:) Contact one of the bureaus once per year and ask for your obligatory free report. Too often credit reports have errors that might adversely affect your score. If there are errors, there are specific procedures to go through to help repair or correct the information.

11) _____ and _____ are two of the best ways of building credit (choose two answers).

   I. Have a checking and savings account
   II. Have good personal references
   III. Piggyback on somebody's good credit
   IIII. Have some debt

   A) I & II
   B) III & IIII
   C) I & III
   D) II & IIII

The correct answer is C:) I & III. Have a checking or savings account and piggyback on somebody's good credit. However, if you plan to piggyback on someone else's good credit, make sure they do indeed have good credit.

12) If you seem to be getting behind on your ability to pay your bills, the best steps to take are _____ and _____.

   A) Seek credit counseling, try to get a short term loan to pay off bills
   B) Cut down on payments, look for an extra job
   C) Hire an attorney, file for Chapter 13 bankruptcy protection
   D) Set up a budget, contact creditors and arrange for a payment plan

The correct answer is D:) Set up a budget, contact creditors and arrange for a payment plan. Always communicate with creditors because it is in both parties interest to work the problems out.

13) A good strategy to follow in regards to credit cards is to

   A) Never use them
   B) Keep the balance below 30%
   C) Only use them in emergencies
   D) Pay off all balances within 30 days

The correct answer is D:) Pay off all balances within 30 days. Most credit cards will charge no interest if charges are paid within 30 days. A credit card is a convenient way to track expenses and provide for smooth cash flow management. Another good strategy is to use a debit card for normal transactions and credit cards only when needed.

14) Credit is a device that causes a lot of stress mainly because

   A) They take advantage of consumer's inability to defer consumption
   B) They allow people to spend more than they are able
   C) They charge exorbitant rates of interest
   D) Too many consumers lack a credit card strategy and discipline

The correct answer is D:) Too many consumers lack a credit card strategy and discipline. Credit cards can provide a valuable tool for expense tracking and cash flow management but their use should be contingent on paying off all charges within the 30 day interest free period.

15) Bankruptcies in the U.S. have declined since 2007 because

   A) Americans are saving more and spending less
   B) Americans have been changing their consumption patterns
   C) The bankruptcy laws were changed to make it more difficult to use bankruptcy protection
   D) Filing fees more than doubled

The correct answer is C:) The bankruptcy laws were changed to make it more difficult to use bankruptcy protection.

16) Which of the following situations would be most ideal?

   A) If a person used their credit card exclusively and always paid minimum monthly payments.
   B) If a person used their credit card to buy only the expensive items they needed and paid as much of the balance that they could at the end of the month. After that they paid minimum payments.
   C) If a person used their credit card regularly, but paid if off at the end of the month to avoid interest.
   D) None of the above

The correct answer is C:) If a person used their credit card regularly, but paid it off at the end of the month to avoid interest.

17) What is home equity?

   A) The market value of the home minus what you owe on it.
   B) What you owe on a home minus what you paid for it.
   C) What you paid for a home minus what you owe on it.
   D) What you owe on a home minus the market value of the home.

The correct answer is D:) What you owe on a home minus the market value of the home.

18) Chapter 20 bankruptcy is a combination of which to types of bankruptcy?

   A) Chapter 9 and Chapter 11
   B) Chapter 7 and Chapter 13
   C) Chapter 7 and Chapter 9
   D) Chapter 9 and Chapter 13

The correct answer is B:) Chapter 7 and Chapter 13. Chapter 7 bankruptcy eliminates portions of a person's debt and then Chapter 13 allows the person to pay off the remaining debt at a manageable rate.

19) Chapter 11 bankruptcy is commonly called

   A) Liquidation
   B) Reorganization
   C) Combination
   D) Wage Earner

The correct answer is B:) Reorganization. This is because in Chapter 11 bankruptcy a person works out a manageable payment plan based on their debt.

20) How is debt-to-income ratio determined?

   A) (Yearly Debt)/(Yearly Income)
   B) (Monthly Income)/(Monthly Debt)
   C) (Yearly Income)/(Yearly Debt)
   D) (Monthly Debt)/(Monthly Income)

The correct answer is D:) (Monthly Debt)/(Monthly Income). Monthly debt involves payment responsibilities such as credit card bills and mortgages, and it is divided by net monthly income.

 Chapter 3 - Let's Go Shopping!

Credit and consumerism have made it possible for the economy to expand and help to improve the standard of living all over the world. For the most part, credit and consumerism are the driving forces of the modern capitalistic society. One could almost say that as a good citizen, it is a major responsibility to consume, which in turn, helps provide employment for others who can then afford to buy the things you produce at your place of work. But let's explore our patriotic duty as members of a capitalistic society: purchasing!

 Truth In Lending and The Consumer Protection Agency

In 1968, congress passed the Truth in Lending Act with the purpose of requiring lenders to disclose all facts and conditions of a loan before it becomes a real transaction. This was done because it was easy to confuse consumers and too many unscrupulous lenders took advantage of the technical complexity of some types of loans. Now, all lenders are required to present simplified disclosers to assure that borrowers are aware of all the loan conditions. However, be prepared to bring out your magnifying glass and review a lot of small print detail. Key things to look for are: the interest rate and penalty sections. Also, recourse for questionable loans can be put into play by contacting the Consumer Protection Agency whose reason for being is to protect consumers.

For most Americans there are normally three large purchases: the home, the car and higher education.

 The Home

Owning your own home demonstrates that you have reached a point in your personal and professional career where you have the economic power to meet the long term responsibility of owning a valuable asset. Not only that, owning has many benefits over renting, but not always.

The simplistic idea is that if you are going to stay in the same place for a long time, buying a home will allow you to do several wonderful things at the same time: pay a lower "rent" in real dollars and the value of property will increase and become an effective hedge against inflation. For the most part, history shows that both these positive effects happen with long term ownership of a home. As a property is paid down over time, equity increases in the property.

For example, if you bought a home ten years ago for $150,000 and during that time the property has increased in estimated market value to $175,000, the owner would increase their equity, which is the sales price less the mortgage loan balance. A renter has no opportunity to build up equity. In fact, as a rental property increases in value, the cost of the rent usually increases as well. This is a major benefit of owning an income producing property. As the owner, the mortgage payment usually stays the same no matter what happens to the value of the property. Considering the fact that most people experience higher incomes over the years, the cost of the mortgage payment will decrease as a percentage of income. Indeed, over time, the payments are made with devaluing money as inflation takes its toll. So, there is a lot to be said for owning a home besides the pride of ownership. On the other hand, given all the associated interest payments, maintenance costs and tax expenses, some real estate experts say that owning a home for less than five years might not make sense. It depends very much on the local real estate market at the time of sale.

The FHA or Federal Housing Administration is a government organization which oversees private housing matters. For example, property standards are determined by the FHA.

The Process of Purchasing a Home

Traditional

When a buyer is not familiar with the area, using a real estate broker is most common. However, it must be kept in mind that these people are sales persons and need you to buy to earn their rather high commissions (normally 6% of the total sales price). As a matter of fact, the real estate agent who represents the buyer can sometimes also represents the needs of the seller to make the deal work. In this way, there may be a slight conflict of interest that the broker must dance around. The value of the broker or their representative is that they are knowledgeable about the market, have access to the Multiple Listings Service (MLS) which lists all of the properties for sale in the area and can help walk the buyer through all the steps of the transaction. The broker assisted sequence of events in purchasing a home are typically the following:

1) The real estate sales person will ask you how much money you can afford to spend on a home. As a general rule, a buyer can afford about 2.5 times their annual salary. So, if you and your spouse make a combined income of $75,000, a home in the $185,000 price range is realistic. At that time, the agent will look through the listings and line up a series of visits to the properties.

2) Once the buyer found a suitable property and has made an offer on a property, the contract is delivered by the realtor to the sellers for acceptance or counter offer.

3) Once an offer is accepted, a contract is signed and an escrow is opened either with a bank or other closing agent. Escrow is a third party account that acts as an objective clearing account for all documents and transfer of funds. At the time of signing, the buyer will usually leave a small non-refundable deposit to "seal the deal."

4) Obtaining financing is the next step. It is the buyer's responsibility to look for financing, usually through a bank or other mortgage lenders. At this point, it is important to find out what terms competitors have. Typically, mortgage terms are composed of:

- A combination of down payment percent of sales price and interest rate. Usually the more the down payment the lower the rate. Also, the term of the loan is important. Most home loans are for 30 years because this makes the monthly payment lower than for shorter term loans. Sometimes referred to as PITI for Payment, Interest, Taxes, Insurance. These items added together makes us the total payment paid every month.
- Lenders may also charge different loan fees called "points" for making the loan. A point is the same as one percentage point.

5) Mortgage payments are set up to pay a more or less constant payment over the life of a loan; however, the front years pay much more in interest so the principle amount of the loan is barely diminished for the first five or so years.

6) Once the buyer chooses the terms that best fit their financial situation, the lender will then begin the process of investigating the credit worthiness of the buyer.

7) The bank needs to not only approve the buyer but also the property as it will act as security (collateral) for the loan. The property is investigated for the correctness of its title and its estimated market value at time of closing. Sometimes a property inspection will be done by a third party. This is usually paid for by the buyer and is not required for a loan.

8) Once all the paperwork has been completed, and the buyer and property approved, it is time for "the closing." At this point, the escrow agent or bank brings both parties together to sign the final documents of title transfer and mortgage loan agreement. The buyer will place the total down payment into the escrow account and the bank will credit the buyer with the mortgage loan amount. From that loan amount, the escrow agent will pay-off any debts on the property and deduct all other closing fees.

Once clear title has been transferred from seller to buyer, the balance of funds in the escrow account will be paid to the seller. Usually, the commission for the real estate broker is also deducted from the escrow account during the closing. After the closing has been completed, the new title and mortgage are registered and formal possession transfers to the new owners. The new owners will most likely open a new escrow account with the bank they financed the home with. This is the account that the property taxes are paid into every month where they are held until the taxes are paid once a year.

The FSBO Process

Over the years, home owners and buyers alike became much more knowledgeable about the home purchase transaction and saw less need for the high commissions paid to real estate agents. A person can do an extensive online search of the area and find out all about the area and what comparative prices are. Many home owners now advertise their own homes without going through an agent. The buyers and/or sellers can contact a closing agent and shop for their own loans. As a matter of fact, most savvy buyers will go to lenders first and find out what size and terms they are qualified for before looking at properties. In other words, they know beforehand what they can afford and don't get caught in the emotional trap of falling in love with a property and then pushing themselves to the financial limit to force the financing to meet the situation.

Contracting a good real estate lawyer and a reputable closing agency is much more cost effective than following the traditional process. Not only can it save the high cost of a realtor but also the closing costs. However, this may not be the best way for first time buyers or buyers who don't have the time to do the due diligence. However, the FSBO sales track is growing rapidly in popularity.

First Time Home Buyers Tax Credit

The hardest part of buying a home is usually coming up with the down payment. To help promote the sales of homes to first time buyers, the U.S. government sometimes offers special tax incentives. This can include tax credits in the year the home is purchased. A tax credit is taken right off the top of any income taxes owed. In effect, a tax credit is much more than it appears. For example, if you are in the 35% tax bracket, the $8,000 credit is actually worth $10,800.

In the past, borrowers have not been very good at saving and lenders took too much risk in allowing low down payments (sometimes as low as zero down). That crisis has changed those liberal lending days and now it will take longer and require more discipline to acquire the necessary down payment. However, there has always been a lot of creativity in finding ways to meet this requirement and many books have been written on the subject.

For example, sellers who are anxious to sell can help make a deal work. You would be surprised how creative financing can be when there is a will to make it work.

 ## Fixed and Adjustable Rate Mortgages

There are two basic types of mortgage rates: fixed rate and adjustable rates.
Fixed rate is when a loan is "locked in" at a certain interest rate for the duration of the loan. The benefit of a fixed rate is that the interest rate won't change over time. On the other hand, an adjustable rate loan usually has an initial lower rate than that of the fixed rate but that rate is adjusted after a specified time. The advantage of an adjustable rate is the initial low interest rate which means lower initial mortgage payments. The disadvantage is that after a time the rate can change and most likely will be an increase in rate and the payment.

 ## Front Loaded Interest

In both types of mortgages, the loan amortization formula provides that for about the first five years or so almost the entire monthly payment is composed of just interest and there is little reduction in the principle of the loan. That is one reason why some people advocate renting rather than buying unless the buyer plans to keep the property for at least five years. The exception to this is when property values are increasing rapidly allowing for equity buildup on the sales side and not by principle pay down.

This sales side equity buildup was partially responsible for the recent real estate crash as speculators jumped in to push prices up and then when the bubble burst they were left owing more on the mortgage than the declining value of the property. This is called being "underwater" meaning that even if the home were sold, the seller would owe more money that the home was worth. Indeed, many underwater speculators just swam away from their loan obligations and left banks holding devalued (toxic) assets which in turn lowered their required asset base and led to the cut-off of lending in general; thus, the credit crisis of recent times.

 Accelerated Mortgage Pay-Down Strategy

If a buyer is planning to keep the property for a long time, some experts promote the idea of paying down the principle by making extra payments to be applied only to the principle. By using this strategy, the amount of interest is reduced over the life of the loan. A similar concept promotes signing up for shorter mortgages. Typically, most buyers sign up for the longest period available because of the lower monthly payment.

To make this point, go to a mortgage calculator like www.homes.com. Let's assume that you want to see the cost of buying a $150,000 home. The terms are 10% down payment and 7% fixed for 30 years. We then select a 15 year loan with the same terms. Select "Amortization schedule" and look at the difference in total interest paid. By paying off the loan in 15 years, you would save $183,934 in interest payments. After 15 years, you would be saving about $1,000 per month for the next 15 years (3 times more than the initial $325 difference in monthly payment). Of course, the longer you go out, the less present value of the money (remember TVM?). Also, notice that the website has a selection "Rent or Buy." This calculation will take all the expense factors and see if it makes more sense to rent or buy.

 Car Purchase

Usually, the second most imposing purchase is buying a car. But this purchase is much less based on cold hard logic and more on emotion and self-image. Most cars are a bad investment but a necessary purchase. That's because most cars lose value do to wear and tear, they also lose value because of the passage of time-unless they become a valuable antique. As cars have a useful life of about six years, the car starts losing value even before it gets off of the sales lot. However, it's a fact that driving is normally a necessity. Many people spend hours per day in their car and are willing to pay a lot of money for comfort and safety. Image is also an important attribute of the car that one buys. A red sports car projects power and sex appeal (look at me), while an expensive, sleek design may exude a different kind of power and success (I am better than you are). Indeed, you are what you drive may be behind the decision of what car to buy.

A little age equals a lot of savings
The idea of being the first owner of a car has a certain appeal. In fact, being the first owner costs several thousand dollars. Because of this, if you want a new car, consider buying a slightly used car. Even just five thousand miles of use will save thousands of

dollars as the rapid depreciation does its work. As most new cars come with at least a 50,000 mile or five year warranty for most factory defects, this is a valuable benefit of buying a new car as car parts and hourly mechanic charges have become expensive. Again, an optimum cost-benefit strategy is to buy a slightly used car with much of the warranty still in place.

But from a more realistic point of view, most car buyers start with the questions: "what can I afford and how much credit can I get?" Typically, most people go into a car dealer and hunt for what they like and then find out what they can afford. As with a home purchase, this impulsive buying can put the buyer in the position of wanting something they can't really afford. The sales person doesn't care because they get paid on the sales price and it is in their best interest to sell you the car with the highest price. As with buying a home, a better strategy is to do the following before starting to look for a car:

1) Find out before you shop for a car how much credit you can expect. Have a dealer or a bank run a credit qualification on you.

2) Go online and look for third party comparisons of different makes and models. These comparisons provide valuable information such as how the car rates on maintenance costs, driving characteristics and other categories of comparison between makes and models. For example www.consumerreport.com is noted for its car comparisons.

3) Once you make a short list of cars within your budget, go to www.bluebook.com. Here you will find the standard industry price ranges for new and used cars.

4) Armed with this knowledge, call around to find out who has the car you are looking for. Be specific but open to what the sales people have to say. But always walk onto a car lot having done your homework first. Once a salesperson hears that you have taken some time to identify what you want they can provide valuable feedback. If you are not an informed buyer, the sales person will usually try to sell you what is best for them; it's just the old "enlightened self-interest" thing that makes capitalism work.

5) If you are buying a car no longer under warranty, find out how much it would cost to purchase a warranty. Take the car to a mechanic of your choosing and have them run a compression and leak test before you buy. Take the car for a drive and run it up to the top of the speed limit and see if there is any shimmying or excessive vibration in the steering wheel. Check the tires for wear. Make sure that you are covered by insurance before doing a test drive.

6) Make sure you and the car are covered to meet all state insurance requirements before driving the new car off the lot.

If you buy a car using credit, expect a 5-10% down payment and the requirement to buy comprehensive property and casualty insurance. Make sure to find out how much this insurance will cost and add it to the annual premium and then divide by 12 months and add it to your monthly payment to see what the total monthly non-operational costs would be. Then figure about 22 cents per mile to drive the car and estimate the number of miles you think you drive in a year. Add all these costs and see how they fit in your budget BEFORE YOU BUY. Not only is it the intelligent thing to do, it will also buy you some time to let the emotion of car buying come down a bit. There are no better retail marketers than car dealers.

Always be ready to walk away. There is always tomorrow and there are always other dealers.

Once you have found a car you would like to buy, ask for the "best price" they can give you. Usually, there won't be much give. But sometimes sales incentives are not just based on price but also on units sold in a specific time period. Sales people and sales managers are driven by their personal sales statistics. If the price doesn't come down much, thank them and give them your telephone number. If they can get you a better price, tell them to call you and you will be right down. Leave. Wait at least three days before making another pass or deciding to buy. Don't be embarrassed; it's just good business practice when dealing with a commodity like an automobile.

 Upside Down and Underwater

Both of these terms refer to the situation where the owner of an car or home has negative equity. For example, you buy a new car but six months later you want to sell the car. When you purchased the car, you put 10% down and have been making payments for six months. You sell the car but when you go to pay off the existing loan, you are shocked to find out that you actually owe more on the car than you thought. Indeed, to pass clear title, you need to pay the finance company more that any equity you might have built up. This situation is referred to as being "upside down" meaning you owe more on the vehicle than it is worth.

As mentioned before, one of the main reasons for the recent credit crisis was the fact that buyers of real estate walked away from their mortgage responsibilities and abandoned their homes because even if they sold their property they couldn't pay off the mortgage balance. This type of loan abandonment was more the result of rapidly falling real estate values. This is called being "underwater" because even if the home were sold, the seller would have to come up with additional funds to pay-off the existing mortgage.

Leasing a Car

During the last few years, leasing a car has become an alternative to owning. However, this is mainly for businesses. The total expenses for a leased car are eligible for business tax deductions and this makes leasing a good alternative for businesses. Of course, if you are an independent contractor and have a formalized business, you can also have your company lease an car. The advantages are not only the payment deductibility but also leasing usually requires less down payment and lower payments. However, like any financed car, full insurance coverage is required.

Education

In today's competitive world, education is a major key to obtaining a good income. Many parents start planning for their children's education from the day the child is born. Understanding how important education is to the person and the nation, governments, both state and federal, have developed programs to help parents save for the ever growing cost of education. Over the past twenty years, the average rate of inflation was about 3% while at the same time the inflation index for education has risen about an average 9%.

Time Value of Money and Planning for Your Children's College Fund

Suppose you and your spouse are expecting your first child. You are still paying off your educational loans and you don't want your child to have the same debt load you took on. So, you start planning for your coming child's education now.

You do some research and find out that the average annual inflation rate for college costs is forecast to be about 9% and you don't think that will change any time soon. So, the question is: how much should you save each year for the next 18 years to build up enough money to pay for your child's future education (Bachelors degree)?

The next step is to decide what universities you might want your child to attend and find out what the annual cost estimate is for tuition, books, room and board. Now, use those cost figures and multiply by the five years it is likely for your child to graduate and come up with a lump sum estimate of today's total costs. Now, you go to the internet and search for "Present Value Calculator" What you want to know is how much you will need to invest today (present value) to come up with the equivalent future amount when it's time for your child to go to college. The "discount rate" you use is the estimated interest rate you would receive on a present value investment over the time period in question. For the purpose of this example, we will assume a 10% return (a shade below the actual average rate of return the general stock market has provided over the last 50 or so years). Let's say that you estimate that you will need $125,000 in today's dollars to pay for your child's bachelor degree. But as this money won't be needed for eighteen years, inflation will make that number much larger. So your investment not only needs to grow but also cover the ravages of inflation over that time period. So, we plug in the numbers.

You find out that $15,500 invested today with an average annual return of 10% (tax free account) will provide for the estimated college costs 18 years in the future. So, you pick up the phone and develop a family "Marketing Plan" to raise the $15,500 to help secure the education of your child. The government offers special tax free savings and investment accounts specifically to help parents plan for the long range educational needs. Don't get confused because you see Present Value $127,121.89. That is telling you within the context of our example that in eighteen years, the present value of your investment will be equal to today's investment of $15,500 if it earns a net return (after all expenses) of 10% annually.

The federal government has enacted a higher education savings plan called a 529 account which provides for tax free savings and investments earmarked for higher education. Many states also have special prepaid programs that for a one time fee guarantees the payment of a child's higher educational costs, usually related to a state chartered university. For example, the state of Florida's Prepaid College Plan offers a range of plans from covering just tuition to total coverage of tuition, books, room and board. Almost all states have similar plans. Of course, the states are just taking the present value lump sum and investing it to cover the estimated future value but with the additional value of a guarantee.

 Financial Aid for Higher Education

Most students won't have the benefit of parents paying for the entire amount, so when it's time to move on to higher education, where do these students turn to help with college costs? Fortunately, there are many believers in education as a benefit to all of society. There are literally millions of websites that help locate educational funding in the form of grants, traineeships, stipends, scholarships, fellowships, and outright loans.

Grants, Scholarships and Fellowships

Usually these programs require no pay back of funds although they do normally have some sort of work requirements. Obtaining these types of assistance is very competitive and requires a long lead time to secure. Allow at least a year for the decision cycle. As each particular program has its own requirements, just locating and applying for these types of no financial liability assistance requires diligence, persistence, and a little luck to land but they are out there in the tens of thousands of opportunity.

The Federal Pell Grant

Federal Pell Grants are direct grants awarded through participating institutions to students with financial need who have not received their first bachelor's degree or who are enrolled in certain post-baccalaureate programs that lead to teacher certification or licensure. These grants are under the U.S. Department of Education and is a needs based program.

Student Loans and Sallie Mae

SLM Corporation, known as Sallie Mae is one of the nation's largest providers and servicers of student loans and handles over $180 billion in student loans to over 10 million borrowers within the U.S. Originally, the government founded Sallie Mae in 1972 to help students pay for college; however, the organization transitioned from a quasi private organization-a GSE (government sponsored entity) into a totally private company in 2004.

According to recent studies, more than 90% of all money borrowed for college fall under the category of a Stafford loan. This loan was first started to help low income families be able to send their children to college. However, overtime these loans have broadened their requirements the two different classes of Stafford loan, unsubsidized and subsidized, have helped to extend its perimeters greatly since its inception in 1965.

Private Loans

Banks understand the importance of higher education and are eager to make educational loans, mainly because they will normally require parental co-signors. Interest rates are not as favorable as the Federal Stafford loans but are readily available.

Loan Forgiveness Programs

The most popular and common loan forgiveness programs are aimed at certain sectors of college graduates: teachers, nurses, and law students who choose to work in high need areas, such as a low income school, medically underserved areas, or as public interest lawyers working with disadvantaged individuals.

Never before has education been so accessible to so many and this has also devalued the value of a university degree. To become competitive, it is becoming necessary to seek an advanced degree or certain expensive technical qualifications such as Microsoft certification. Indeed, education doesn't cease after graduation. Often times, people need to upgrade their skills or they become less competitive. Sometimes, employers offer educational assistance but working a full time job and going to school can be too high a price to pay and it is only a reasonable goal when the employee is out of a job. Now they have the time, but not the money – the old "catch-22."

Perhaps more than ever in today's changing economic environment, continual or periodic education is a must and it is important to keep this in mind. Fortunately, tax deferred pension plans allow for funds to be withdrawn for educational needs and educational needs should be an important part of your budgeting as we will discuss in the chapter on Investing. But let's say it here: at a minimum, at least 10% of your income should be automatically put into a tax deferred pension plan.

Military Educational Benefits

After graduation from high school, many students don't know what they want to study and yet they aren't really very employable. A good alternative for many students would be to join a branch of the military. Not only does the military provide recent grads with a good transition from family to independent life experience, but it also exposes young adults to the world of responsibility and accountability. But here is the real good news: after serving with a branch of the military, the ex-soldier is eligible for the G.I. bill, which provides funding for education. Indeed, it is similar to receiving a partial scholarship for higher education. Not only that, for qualifying students, the military will pay for medical school in exchange for a seven year commitment as a doctor in one of the military branches.

 Make Your Own Scholarship

Some companies encourage and help with tuition for employees seeking continuing education. But even if your company does not offer such assistance, an enterprising employee with a vision for the future might very well propose a plan to their employer where the employee and employer split the cost of mutually beneficial education or training. Almost everybody will agree that one of the best investments one can make is in education and in oneself.

To summarize, in today's world, education is important and ongoing; it doesn't stop after graduation. Parents have a certain defacto obligation to plan and provide for at least a university degree for their children, but life-long learning will be on the shoulders of the children themselves. Education and ever advancing skill sets are important factors for financial survival in the modern economy. More and more specialized knowledge is for sale and the wise person will include ongoing educational costs not only for their children but also for themselves.

Sample Test Questions - Chapter 3

1) Home equity is

   A) The concept that all people should be able to own a home
   B) The difference between the sales price and the down payment
   C) The difference between the value of the home and the balance of the mortgage
   D) The equity in a home is the same as years of ownership

The correct answer is C:) The difference between the value of the home and the balance of the mortgage. There are two ways to increase equity: increasing asset value and pay down of loan principle.

2) If the sales price of a home is $180,000 and the down payment required is 10%, the mortgage would be based upon

   A) $198,000
   B) $180,000
   C) $162,000
   D) $18,000

The correct answer is C:) $162,000. 10% of the sale price would be $18,000 leaving $162,000 to be financed.

3) Typically, the broker's commission on an $180,000 home would be

   A) $18,000
   B) $2,000
   C) $4,000
   D) $10,800

The correct answer is D:) $10,800. In most of the country, 6% commission is standard but the commission rate is always negotiable.

4) FSBO means

   A) Foreclosure standard buy out
   B) Family style build out
   C) For sale by owner
   D) Family subsidy borrowing option

The correct answer is C:) For sale by owner. This is a growing trend mainly because more and more buyers and sellers are familiar with the process of research, negotiation and how to outsource escrow and legal services.

5) As a rule of thumb, a multiple of _____ times total annual income would equal the highest priced home a buyer should consider buying.

   A) 3.0
   B) 4.0
   C) 5.0
   D) 2.5

The correct answer is D:) 2.5. For example, if you and your spouse make a combined annual income of $100,000 you should limit to a top price of $250,000.

6) During the pay down of a mortgage, the _____ year's payments are almost entirely made up of interest with little pay down of the mortgage balance.

   A) First five or so
   B) Middle
   C) Final five
   D) The even

The correct answer is A:) First five or so.

7) Many experts say that unless you plan to live at least _____ in the location, you are probably wiser to rent.

   A) 5 years
   B) 18 months
   C) 3 years
   D) 1 year

The correct answer is A:) 5 years. As the first five or so years payments are mostly made up of interest, unless the value of the property has gone up a certain amount, selling the property may end up with a net loss because of the expenses that in effect reduce any equity build up.

8) Before shopping for a home, it's a good idea to

   A) Seek credit counseling first
   B) Make sure you can pay at least 20% of the purchase price
   C) Pre-qualify for the amount of credit you can expect
   D) Find a qualified co-signer

The correct answer is C:) Pre-qualify for the amount of credit you can expect. By doing this, you can help provide some discipline instead of letting emotions dictate how much you are willing versus how much you can spend.

9) Car loans usually have higher interest rates because

   A) Cars don't hold their value and they are a mobile asset subject to accidents and theft
   B) Cars are easy to steal or hide and they have maintenance costs
   C) Cars can be walked away from both physically and financially
   D) Cars loans have a higher delinquency rate and have higher transaction costs

The correct answer is A:) Cars don't hold their value and they are a mobile asset subject to accidents and theft.

10) Before going to look at cars, it is a good idea to

    A) Ask others what they think is a good car to buy
    B) Ask several mechanics what they think is a good car to buy
    C) Consult an industry trade publication
    D) Go online and look for car comparisons done by third party experts

The correct answer is D:) Go online and look for car comparisons done by third party sources.

11) If you finance an car, you should be aware that

    A) The lender will require that you be at least 21 years old with good credit
    B) If you are under 21 years old, you will require a co-signer on the loan
    C) You will be required to carry the full insurance coverage
    D) The car is required to have a maintenance check every 3,000 miles

The correct answer is C:) You will be required to carry the full insurance coverage. As the car is the security for the loan, the lender wants protection against loss or liabilities associated with the car.

12) One of the best ways to save for education is to

   A) Have a separate savings account for education
   B) Invest in stocks and bonds
   C) Make regular deposits to a taxable pension plan
   D) Enroll in a state sponsored education savings plan or purchase zero coupon bonds early in the child's life and place them in a tax sheltered education savings account

The correct answer is D:) Enroll in a state sponsored education savings plan or purchase zero coupon bonds early in the child's life and place them in a tax sheltered education savings account.

13) If you find out that the student loans will not be enough to cover your estimated expenses you should

   A) Look for a part time job
   B) Enlist with a branch of the military and plan on using the G.I. bill when you finish your service
   C) Look online for sources of grants, scholarships and other forms of educational financial assistance
   D) Contact the private lenders

The correct answer is C:) Look online for sources of grants, scholarships and other forms of educational financial assistance.

14) As a student, if you aren't sure of what career you want to study, a good course of action would be to

   A) Join a branch of the military after making sure what the qualifications are for the G.I. Bill
   B) Seek job counseling and testing to see where your interests and abilities might match a certain professional profile
   C) Read widely about what jobs will be in demand in the future
   D) All of the above

The correct answer is D:) All of the above. Too many families work hard and sacrifice to assure a proper education for their children but fail to do the work to find a good match for the student. What we need to keep in mind is that many of the best jobs are not that well known. It takes research and time to find the best match. Start by finding out what talents and interests a student has and find a good match. Indeed, if you like what you are doing, your chances of success are hig, no matter what field.

15) There are numerous sources for educational funding. All things being equal, obtaining a _____ is the most preferable.

   A) Government sponsored student loan
   B) Bank loan
   C) Family loan
   D) Grant

The correct answer is D:) Grant. A grant is an outright gift to qualified applicants and usually requires no financial pay back.

16) Who pays the real estate agent's commission?

   A) Buyer
   B) Seller
   C) Buyer and seller combined
   D) None of the above

The correct answer is B:) Seller. The real estate agent doesn't receive any payment until the home is sold and it is the seller's responsibility to pay their commission.

17) What is the minimum down payment needed to avoid mortgage insurance?

   A) 10%
   B) 15%
   C) 20%
   D) 35%

The correct answer is C:) 20%. For a person buying a $300,000 home, this means they would need to pay $60,000 up front to avoid PMI.

18) Which government administration oversees private housing matters?

   A) FTC
   B) REIT
   C) FHA
   D) FDIC

The correct answer is C:) FHA. The FHA is the Federal Housing Administration and oversees private housing matters. For example, property standards are determined by the FHA.

Chapter 4 - Taxes

We've all heard the old saying, "Nothing is for sure except death and taxes." Well, recent advances in genetics might make death obsolete someday. But not taxes. For a civilization to function somebody needs to pay for the governing infrastructure or chaos will reign. At least that's the understanding. However, taxes have become a constant topic of controversy. Indeed, taxation may become the defining factor for the future shape of the U.S. economy and culture. More people expect more from the government but are unwilling to pay for it in the form of taxes. The real problem is that governments by their very nature are interested in their agenda and not that of the people for whom they are supposed to serve. Graft, corruption and incompetence have made the citizenry skeptical about the cost-benefit of taxes and these concerns make it difficult for government to raise taxes in fear of a taxpayer revolt. As a result of this stalemate, citizens now pay high taxes but get little from the government.

The Internal Revenue Service (IRS) is the responsible agency for the definition, regulation and collection of taxes. The U.S. Tax Code is over 4,000 pages and its complexity and force majeure is the cause of concern for all citizens. Entire industries such as the legal services and accounting attract billions of dollars spent on these services are centered on ways to maneuver around this obtuse set of tax regulations. On the other hand, taxes are important tools to help direct the economic policies of the U.S.

But let there be no doubt, citizens don't like paying taxes, particularly when they constantly question the use of the funds. For one thing, unlike the state governments, the Federal government is not subject to the constraints of meeting a budget.

Income Taxes

If you are a regular employee, your taxes are taken directly out of your paycheck. You can change what amounts are taken out of your check by changing your deductions. The best possible scenario is to break even at the end of the year or owe a small amount. That way you have control of your money for the entire year, but you won't get a big check back at tax time.

W-2 Status

A regular employee is classified as a "W-2" employee, which is named after the form regular employees receive at the end of the tax year stating all of the taxes the employer has taken out of their paychecks. Sometimes the amount taken out is more than required for the employee and they can receive a refund or sometimes the employee will owe more taxes than have already been taken out and will need to pay additional taxes. Each regular employee is required to fill out a W-4 form which allows the employee to stipulate how much taxes they wish to have taken out of their paychecks in accordance with the IRS code. Some workers may have some allowable deductions such as the interest on a home mortgage which will allow an employee to have fewer taxes taken out of their paycheck.

1099 Status

A worker who is not a regular employee but performs contract work for a company is considered a "1099" employee, also named after the IRS form applicable for the contractor status. These contract workers have no taxes withheld from the gross pay. It becomes the responsibility of the 1099 contract worker to pay the proper amount of taxes within the proper time limits. In addition, the IRS requires that employers collect information on contractors by filling in a form W-9. This helps act as a cross check to make sure that a 1099 contractor pays taxes. An important point is that only regular W-2 employees are eligible for company fringe benefits whereas contract employees are not.

Individual income tax rates are "progressive" in that the more income a person makes, the higher the percent of that income goes to income taxes. Of course, wealthy people are also capable of hiring smart lawyers and accountants to help protect them from taxation. During those years of high tax brackets, special tax code "loop holes" were slipped into the code which protected the rich to the point that many of the "high bracket" taxpayers paid little or no income taxes. Indeed, even today some of the wealthiest individuals and companies pay little or no taxes.

Taxes are figured from what is called adjusted taxable Income. For individuals, this is computed on the IRS 1040 Individual Income Tax form. Basically, a regular employee would use the company provided W-2 and all other sources of income and then deduct those allowable amounts as specified in the IRS tax code. Once all forms of taxable income have been adjusted where possible, the amount at the end of the process becomes the adjusted taxable income from which taxes are paid if not already taken out in payroll withholding by the employer.

A 1040EZ is used for individuals who have a very simple return. For example, if an individual has wages from salary and takes only the standard deductions, they are able to use this form. If an individual needs to itemize or has other types of income, they must use a 1040. The 1040A is a step between the 1040 and the 1040EZ. It can handle slightly more.

Form 1040A is a shorter form than the traditional 1040 income tax return form. It can be used if a person made less than $100,000 and takes the standard deduction.

Form 1040X is used to make corrections to previously filed forms.

Other Payroll Taxes

As mentioned previously, in regards to regular employees, employers are charged with the responsibility of withholding (confiscating) income taxes from an employee paycheck. But there are other taxes that are also collected each pay period by the employer. These other taxes are:

- Federal income tax withholding (based on withholding tables)
- F.I.C.A. withholding. FICA is an acronym for the Federal Insurance Contributions Act. There are three component taxes for FICA: Social Security, Medicare and disability insurance.
- Social Security tax withholding (6.25% up to the annual maximum income of $106,600). The employer is required to contribute half and the employee an equal portion for a total of 12.5% of wages. The amount withheld is the emp l o y e e contribution.
- Medicare tax withholding (1.45%).
- Disability insurance depends on state law.
- State income tax withholding-if appropriate.

April 15th

At the end of each calendar year, every person who has made over $500 must file an individual income tax report called the 1040 Individual Income Tax form. This form must be sent in before midnight of April 15th for the past tax year. Keep in mind that it is a violation of federal law not to file an annual income tax form. However, it is not against the law to not pay taxes by that time. After April 15th, all unpaid taxes accrue interest and penalties. The IRS has the authority to inspect all backup documentation and determine the correct amount of taxes due. Indeed, if a case of tax evasion can be proven, the IRS has the right to confiscate and liquidate assets to pay off delinquent taxes. In some cases, citizens can be sent to jail for violations of the tax code.

Estimated Taxes

Estimated taxes are taxes that are paid based on income that was not subject to withholding. For example, if a person rents their basement the taxes are not automatically taken out of it like they would be on a paycheck. Reported taxes are taxes paid based on the taxable income a person reports on their income tax return form. These forms can be amended, and then they would have amended taxes.

 Sample Test Questions - Chapter 4

1) The government agency in charge of enforcing the tax code is the

   A) Internal Reserve System
   B) Treasury Department
   C) IRT
   D) Internal Revenue Service

The correct answer is D:) Internal Revenue Service.

2) All people who make over $500 within a tax year must file a form _____ before midnight of _____.

   A) 1120, April 1 of the following year
   B) 1040, April 15th of the following year
   C) 1040, April 15th of the same year
   D) None of the above

The correct answer is B:) 1040, April 15th of the following year.

3) Every employee eligible for company benefits are normally required to have filled out which form?

   A) 1040
   B) W-1
   C) 1099
   D) W-4

The correct answer is D:) W-4.

4) If you and your spouse file a joint 1040 tax form and you each made $35,000 the past tax year, your tax bracket is most likely to be

   A) 10-15%
   B) 25-35%
   C) 25%
   D) 35%

The correct answer is C:) 25%. Filing a joint tax return usually provides for lower tax on both combined income versus each filing as a single tax payer.

5) Social security tax is a co-pay tax whereby the employee pays half and the employer pays half. On the typical W-2 pay check, _____ percent of income will be withheld for the company paid portion.

   A) 10
   B) 12.5
   C) 6.2
   D) 1.4

The correct answer is C:) 6.2. Social Security taxes are based on the first $106,600 of income.

6) A 1099 employee refers to someone who works on a _____ basis.

   A) Part time
   B) Full time but without benefits
   C) Contract
   D) Full time

The correct answer is C:) Contract. IRS code specifies what constitutes a 1099 employee. Contract employees are responsible for their own tax liabilities and the company has no liability to make standard tax withholdings form payments to a 1099 employee.

7) By using specified _____, income tax liability can be reduced.

   A) Expenses
   B) Sources of income
   C) Dependents
   D) Deductions

The correct answer is D) Deductions. There are standard deductions such as number of dependents, mortgage interest and other defined expenses that qualify as deductions.

8) Perhaps the greatest obstacles to implementing a one bracket flat tax are _____ and _____.

   A) Lawyers, accountants
   B) Distrust of the federal government , excessive military spending
   C) Bracket creep, corruption
   D) Lower income earners, charities

The correct answer is A:) Lawyers, accountants. Helping clients to strategize ways to avoid paying taxes forms the central part of the accounting profession as well as the legal profession. By simplifying the tax laws, these professions would take a big hit. Of course, it cuts both ways as these professionals are highly paid and pay a significant amount of income taxes.

9) As a general rule, there is constant upward pressure to increase taxes because the nature of government bureaucracies is to _____ and push the limits of the _____.

   A) Become corrupt, law
   B) Grow, budget
   C) Grow, ethics
   D) Become inefficient, budget

The correct answer is B:) Grow, budget. Organizational behavior recognizes that it is not in the organizations best interest to stay within budgets as the budget will only be cut to try to force more efficiency. Also, power has a tendency to constantly seek a larger base.

10) One way to reduce the need for more government revenues yet provide essential services is to _____ services that can be made profitable.

   A) Increase the cost of
   B) Eliminate
   C) Privatize
   D) Market

The correct answer is C:) Privatize. The idea is that if a service is in demand for only a certain segment of a society, let those people pay for those needed services. Governments should stick to providing for the common good.

11) According to one saying "The power to tax is the power to…"

   A) Provide for the common good
   B) Maintain a powerful military
   C) Create a better future
   D) To destroy

The correct answer is D:) To destroy. Sometimes taxation can be abused and destroy a delicate economy.

12) Under the law, not filing a _____ is worse than not paying taxes.

   A) W-2
   B) Tax waiver
   C) 1040 by December 31st
   D) 1040 by April 15th of the following year

The correct answer is D:) 1040 by April 15th of the following year. Not paying taxes on time incurs penalties and fees. Not checking in with Uncle Sam raises red flags.

13) A tax that increases with income is called a _____ tax. A tax that is the same for all income levels is called a _____ tax.

   A) Scaled, flat
   B) Regressive, progressive
   C) Bracket, sales
   D) Progressive, regressive

The correct answer is D:) Progressive, regressive. Using a universal sales tax as used in many places in Europe has not been as well accepted because it affectively is a regressive tax in that it penalizes people who make less income because it is a higher percentage of income as compared to a lower percentage for higher income levels.

14) The perpetual breaking of budgets and increasing national debt will most likely end up being revealed in

   A) Deflation as prices come down
   B) Inflation as the U.S. dollar decreases in value and imports become more expensive
   C) The U.S. will have a difficult time selling its bonds to overseas buyers
   D) The dollar will crash and the U.S. economy will tank

The correct answer is B:) Inflation as the U.S. dollar decreases in value and imports become more expensive.

15) Even though most people don't like paying taxes, it is against the law to

　　A) Publicly complain
　　B) Not pay taxes
　　C) Not file a W-2
　　D) Not file a 1040

The correct answer is D:) Not file a 1040.

16) What is the difference between tax credits and tax deductions?

　　A) Tax credits reduce the tax by an amount and tax deductions are proportional to taxable income.
　　B) Tax deductions reduce the tax by an amount and tax credits are proportional to taxable income.
　　C) Tax credits increase taxes and deductions decrease taxes proportional to taxable income.
　　D) Tax credits increase taxes and deductions decrease taxes by a specific amount.

The correct answer is A:) Tax credits reduce the tax by an amount and tax deductions are proportional to taxable income. For example, for a person in the 25% tax bracket a $100 tax credit would reduce the amount by $100 whereas the same amount in a tax deduction would reduce it by only $25.

17) Which of the following most correctly describes the 1040A income tax form?

　　A) It is a shortened version of the regular 1040 form for people who take the standard deduction.
　　B) It is an expanded version of the regular 1040 form for people who wish to itemize their deductions.
　　C) It is used for people to make corrections to their previously filed forms.
　　D) None of the above

The correct answer is A:) It is a shortened version of the regular 1040 form for people who take the standard deduction.

18) Which of the following most correctly describes the 1040X income tax form?

   A) It is a shortened version of the regular 1040 form for people who take the standard deduction.
   B) It is an expanded version of the regular 1040 form for people who wish to itemize their deductions.
   C) It is used for people to make corrections to their previously filed forms.
   D) None of the above

The correct answer is C:) It is used for people to make corrections to their previously filed forms. The form looks essentially the same as a 1040 form, but with 3 columns; one with the original value, one with the change and one with the new value.

19) Which government administration oversees economic concerns such as keeping the market free and fair?

   A) FTC
   B) REIT
   C) FHA
   D) FDIC

The correct answer is A:) FTC. The FTC is the Federal Trade Commission and regulates business practices to ensure that the market remains free, fair and competitive

 # Chapter 5 - Financial Planning

As mentioned in the first chapter, if you want to go from A to B it is a good idea to have a map that shows how to get there. If you want to have a solid financial future, you also need a financial map on how to get there. And, of course, define where "there" is. Most people think that getting that good job is financial planning. That is far from the truth. If income is not guarded and nurtured, expenses will eat up every available dollar. Planning and discipline is a must and should be part of a person's everyday life, no matter the level of income.

 ## Creating Wealth

First of all, you need to establish a budget which tracks all income and expenses. At a minimum, income needs to match living expenses. Once income exceeds living expenses, there comes the opportunity to either improve the quality of life or to build wealth. Unfortunately, the two choices are usually mutually exclusive. The choice of whether or not to spend or save becomes a constant battle between the seduction of short term gratification or long term wealth building. After you read this chapter, you will most likely find the logic to help stave off the temptations of living in a glitzy consumer society, at least partially. What remarkable observations could persuade a consumer, money or plastic in hand, to opt out of spending and "lose the fun of buying" just to watch the money turn into some digit on an account statement? What's the fun in that?

What if someone told you that with some spare income, some early planning and long term discipline, you could become a millionaire within 35 years-with a fairly high degree of probability and a fairly low degree of sacrifice or risk? Does this sound like snake oil?

As usual, a picture is worth a thousand words-in this case a chart and a calculation- so let's take a look at the following real world example.

First, some assumptions:

- You are 21 years old
- You have enough extra income to invest (save) $2000 annually
- You invest your annual $2,000 in a tax deferred investment account in a stock market index and make no withdrawals
- The average rate of return over the next 35 years is 12%-the historical average of the stock market index for the past fifty years or so.

Keep in mind that there are many types of investments and strategies which a professional financial planner or investment advisor can recommend. Many people think that they can make investment choices for themselves; however, unless you have put in the time and study of this vast and complex field, you are probably better off to seek out professional advice, particularly for long term investing. Indeed, long term investing is just that, investing. Short term investing is really speculation and involves much greater risk and reward. Passive, long term investing does not require constant monitoring and usually an annual review of your portfolio (a mixture of investments) is all that is needed. The scope of this book does not begin to explain how to invest. But, what is vital is to understand the promise of regular long term investment-particularly starting at an early age.

The Power of Tax Free Compounding Investment

So, at the age of 56, you are a millionaire without lifting a finger! It sounds too good to be true, right? All it takes is a disciplined system of savings and long term investments in solid companies or just a stock market index fund. So why don't more people follow this simple plan? Because of lack of knowledge about the power of compounding gains, lack of discipline and patience.

Now that you know, the burden of becoming a millionaire is now on you. Ignorance is no longer an excuse. Keep in mind that this all takes place with passive income only. You can still have fun just as long as you make sure your long term investment plan is being funded and followed. Consider this: if you go out to a restaurant once a week and spend an average of $30 each visit, you would spend $1560 per year. Add in the tips and you are almost there for your $2,000 annual contribution. And, of course, the more money you contribute to your long term plan, the faster you become a millionaire or the more money you have when it comes time to start taking distributions. However, when you take the money out and turn it into real income really determines the realized returns on your investments.

Establishing Financial Priorities

Needless to say, as your life progresses and changes, so do your priorities. But the financial realities of survival form the base of financial planning. For example, there are basic needs such as food, shelter and health. Within those needs is the freedom to choose the level satisfaction of those needs. You can eat rice and beans and live in a shack or you can live in a mansion on the beach. However, those lifestyle choices depend on the economics, needs and desires of the individual.

So the basic needs are filtered through each individual's decision on what lifestyle they want and how much they are capable or willing to pay. This balance of income and realistically achievable lifestyle forms the basis of the all important budget. Indeed, many prefer to spend what might be savings on maintaining a certain lifestyle. However, prudence dictates that there is some attention to the potential for "rainy days." As more of society prefers to focus only on maintaining or achieving a certain lifestyle, more pressure is being put on government to provide for emergency assistance when poor planning finds families and individuals without the finances to meet the unexpected. This lack of financial planning has a weakening effect on the notion of a free and responsible democratic society. So, lifestyle choices should also account for not burdening the society in case of misfortune. With that in mind, let's look at how a realistic budget should be structured so as to make sure that the risk of financial catastrophe can be avoided or at least minimized.

 ## *Budgeting Considerations*

Income
- Productive (employment)
- Passive (savings and investment)

Expenses
- *Living expenses:* includes the basics but incorporates the quality and expense related to each expense
- *Life insurance:* insures the family income earners incase of loss of in come
- *Disability insurance:* income protection in case of incapacitation
- *Medical insurance:* health care protection (Long Term Care insurance becomes a concern as one gets older. This type of insurance provides for elder care or any catastrophic illness that requires long term, expensive care)
- *Emergency living expenses* (at least 4 months required cash flow)

Disposable income is total net income less all expenses
- A percentage goes to long term wealth building
- A percentage to other financial-personal goals

The italicized factors need further explanations. If those factors are not planned for, there could be exposure to catastrophic events that would put tremendous stress and need at the worst possible time. These factors should be considered before funding the disposable income line item.

Life Insurance

There are basically two types of life insurance: term and whole life.

Term insurance is the least expensive insurance in that you pay a premium just for the death benefit. Term insurance is not considered an investment but merely the cost of protection. Like all life insurance death benefits, the payout is tax free. The price of the insurance (premium) increases with age and medical profile; however, it is possible to buy a level premium (same price) over a specified period of time.

Whole life insurance provides two benefits: an interest bearing savings account on a portion of the premiums paid and a death benefit. Due to commissions and other management fees, whole life usually provides for less death benefit and a higher premium. However, for some situations, whole life is the appropriate product.

Insurance is a wonderful product when you need it. But many types of insurance are complex and have built in charges and fees that need to be considered before purchasing any policy. For example, there are insurance products such as *fixed and variable annuities*, which are hybrids of insurance and investment products. These contracts can be very complex and have built in fees that need to be analyzed carefully.

Insurances of all types are considered so important and complex that each state has a special office of insurance regulation dedicated to regulating insurance in the particular state. Indemnity is when a person is not responsible for any damages or losses are suffered. Most often the term is used in terms of insurance. An insurance company indemnifies the policy holder.

Liability Insurance

Liability Insurance is a necessary consideration for providers of products or services which can leave the insured open to law suits for professional misconduct. Typically, doctors, lawyers, certain types of engineers and almost all businesses usually have some form of liability insurance. For example, restaurants usually have coverage for customer food poisoning, slipping, chipped teeth, etc. Indeed, all motorists in all states are required to have liability insurance in cases they become involved in an accident.

Disability Insurance

Disability Insurance comes in three basic forms: workers compensation, company benefit or private policy.

- Workers compensation is usually a requirement for employers. If a worker gets injured while on the job, the state workers compensation fund will pay for medical costs and a certain amount for disability. If a worker becomes permanently injured while on the job, Social Security programs provide for financial assistance. However, workers compensation is only job related.

- Many companies offer sick pay coverage that usually covers a limited number of days or pay periods.

- Insurance companies offer disability policies that cover specific time periods and payouts. This type of policy can be particularly important for independent contractors who must work to produce income. If, for some reason they become disabled, having disability insurance can be a real safety net, at least for a period of time. Indeed, emergency funds and disability insurance should be a major consideration when setting up a budget.

COBRA

COBRA stands for The Comprehensive Omnibus Budget Reconciliation Act. It requires employers to allow employees to retain medical insurance after they quit or are terminated, for up to 18 months. It gives workers and their families who lose their health benefits the right to choose to continue group health benefits provided by their group health plan for limited periods of time under certain circumstances such as voluntary or involuntary job loss, reduction in the hours worked, transition between jobs, death, divorce, and other life events. Qualified individuals may be required to pay the entire premium for coverage up to 102 percent of the cost to the plan.

COBRA generally requires that group health plans sponsored by employers with 20 or more employees in the prior year offer employees and their families the opportunity for a temporary extension of health coverage (called continuation coverage) in certain instances where coverage under the plan would otherwise end.

COBRA outlines how employees and family members may elect continuation coverage. It also requires employers and plans to provide notice.

HIPAA

The Health Insurance Portability and Accountability Act (HIPAA) provides rights and protections for participants and beneficiaries in group health plans. HIPAA includes protections for coverage under group health plans that limit exclusions for preexisting conditions; prohibits discrimination against employees and dependents based on their health status; and allows a special opportunity to enroll in a new plan to individuals in certain circumstances. HIPAA may also give you a right to purchase individual coverage if you have no group health plan coverage available, and have exhausted COBRA or other continuation coverage.

Medical Insurance

Unfortunately, the cost of medical services of all types has escalated rapidly. Those people who usually have medical insurance are usually part of a group where the costs are spread out over a large population of premium payers. However, for individuals, obtaining a private health care policy is costly. Two important parts of health insurance are:

- *Portability:* If you leave an employer who offers health insurance, you can transfer your existing health care plan with you.
- *Denial of coverage:* As individuals applying for health coverage, each applicant is assessed as to the risk to the insurance company. If there are any indications that the client might actually need current or future medical care, insurance companies can either simply deny coverage or offer a very expensive premium.

Emergency Living Expenses

There are many "acts of god" or misfortunes that can befall a person and not be covered by insurance. As a general rule, it's a good idea to have at least 4 months living expenses immediately available for the unexpected. But the sad fact is, that without the other insurances discussed before, only savings and other assets can be looked to for relief from the unexpected. Of course, there are other recourses such as family, friends, charities, and some government assistance. However, in financial planning, consideration must be given to the exposure to all potential risks.

In summary, before deciding on what you consider as disposable income, consider the need for protection not only for your own protection but also of your assets that could be exposed to liabilities.

There are many books, articles and professional financial planners available to help with the details of financial planning. The worker mentality of just being able to pay the bills will not take you where you want to go-in fact, you need to start by defining where it is you want to go! By planning, you become proactive. By not planning, you are reactive and much more vulnerable. Take your life into your own hands by planning-both financial and personal- as they are closely linked.

Simple steps to becoming proactive in your financial life:

- Think of where you want to be both personally and financially within the next 1, 5, and 20 years. Write it down. Don't worry about accuracy. Think in general terms.
- Think of ways to get there. If you don't know, start to do some research. Talk to people who have achieved what it is you want to achieve. Read biographies and self help books. Once you have an idea, write it down.
- Identify special skills needed and how they can be acquired. Find out how much it costs. Write it down.
- Make a budget. Write it down and follow it.
- Create disposable income either by increasing income or reducing expenses.
- The first "expense" you pay is for projected disposable income (savings, investment funds).
- Start a program of long term investing with a portion of disposable income.
- Think of what skills or education can help reach your goals. Save a portion of your disposable income to obtain the needed training.
- Always observe your budget and avoid getting into debt unless it makes financial sense and does not make you vulnerable to the potential excessive liability.
- Always remember that the unexpected can happen to you.
- Connect your short range planning with your long range planning. With a plan and daily discipline you can reach your goals, but it takes patience and discipline.
- Picture yourself as reaching your goals. Know it will happen if you follow your plan. Be positive and don't focus too much on the negative.
- Don't be afraid to change your plans. If it doesn't feel right or make sense anymore, cut your losses and make the changes needed. Always be moving ahead. You and your goals will change over time.

Investing Overview

Long term investing is basically defined as holding an investment for more than 5 years with the expectation of increasing value of the stock and the opportunity to collect dividends if applicable. When investors look to short term investing where they hold a stock or investment for less than a few years or even months, that activity is speculation and should be left to the experts and risk takers.

The main parameter considered in investing and speculating is the risk-reward of an investment; the higher the risk, the higher the reward. For long term investors, the preferred strategy is for lower risk-reward investments but with the goal of letting the power of compounding gains provide the reward over time. While there are a wide range of investments, the long term investor plans to make the core of the portfolio (a range of different investments) focused mainly on low risk-reward investments. An additional way to reduce risk is through diversification by holding different types of assets. For example, a portfolio might contain a certain mix of equities (stocks and bonds), real estate, commodities (precious metals) and cash. The mix and percentage depends of each asset depends on many things that a professional investment advisor can help evaluate.

The Risk-Reward Pyramid

The risk-reward pyramid has been created by the investment industry to give a general picture of the levels of risk and reward for the most common types of passive investments. Passive income means that you don't do any work. But don't be fooled, learning the intricacies of investing is hardly passive. Unless you have time and the interest, you are much better off to seek professional guidance when making investments.

Later in this chapter, you will see that one of the best investments from a risk-reward point of view is developing your own business. Even though about 80% of new businesses aren't in business for longer than five years, this active investment of time and assets is the main creator of wealth in the U.S. The typical path is to get an education or skill, become expert in your field and then either start or buy a business. With an active investment, you are always there putting your own money at risk and as a result make every attempt to make it work. Passive investments, on the other hand, depends on the success of others and the only real control an investor has is to either buy or sell and it becomes the job of the professional financial advisor to help you, the client, determine which investment is best for you. Some will require you to monitor the investment and others will do it for you, for a nice commission.

 Typical Goals and Investment Vehicles

SHORT TERM GOALS (1-3 years): down payment for a home, car, vacation, consumer items, education, hobbies.

For short term goals, you normally will not use tax deferred investments because of the tax consequences for early withdrawal of funds. So, you will want to invest for the short term in a fairly liquid investment with few restrictions. Some typical types of short term investments are:

1. **Savings account:** Today, the interest rates earned on a savings account is very low but the money is liquid and secure. This investment has very low risk-low reward.

2. **Money Market Account:** This type of account is a good substitute for savings in that it is liquid and usually pays a bit higher return than a standard interest bearing savings account. Basically a very conservative mutual fund, the only difference between it and a savings account is that the shares must be redeemed first and this usually takes several working days for the liquidation.

3. **Short Term Certificate of Deposit (CD):** A little higher interest than savings, but has the same level of security. However, some CDs can have early withdrawal fees. This investment has low risk-low reward.

4. **Bonds:** These are basically an IOU which pays regular interest and then the initial investment is paid back at the specified date. The risk depends largely on the issuer and their ability to make the payments and pay back the principal. However, bonds can assume a higher risk reward profile if they are traded and not just held to maturity. If a company goes bankrupt, bond holders have access to the company assets for recourse. On the other hand, a **debenture** is similar to a bond but has no recourse to company assets in case of a default. A common practice is that companies that issue bonds be required to have a **sinking fund** where the borrowers are required to make regular contributions to help assure investors that future interest payments on the bonds will be paid. Callable bonds are bonds which the issuer can redeem before the specified date.

5. **Mutual funds:** These are managed investments in a basket of different types of stocks, bonds, currencies, and commodities. This diversification is what lowers the risk from just owning individual issues. Most banks offer mutual funds as do the brokerages. These are riskier but can have higher rewards. Most experts would say that for short term investors, these may not be the best because of the

subscription and management fees. However, there are many "no load" mutual funds that charge low fees and no subscription. This investment has higher risk of losing capital than 1, 2 & 3 but with potentially higher rewards.

6. **Individual stocks:** These instruments are a primary way for companies to raise capital. Some companies offer to pay dividends to stock holders but more and more just the potential of an increase in stock valuation is enough to attract investors. There are many subcategories of stocks and ways to invest in the stock markets. The stock markets in general (there are over 25 major stock exchanges throughout the world) as an index have shown the ability to provide an average rate of return that is well above the average rate of inflation (for example, companies listed on the New York Stock exchange have shown an average annual stock value appreciation of about 12% for the past 60 years. However, history is no guarantee of the future. Churning is when a broker buys large amounts of stock to get a commission, even though it is not in the customer's best interest.

7. **Commodities:** These investments deal with a wide range of basic resources such as food products, timber, minerals, oil, energy and over 50 other basic raw materials. Commodities are considered even more speculative than stocks.

8. **Entrepreneurial activities:** You might find an activity that derives income from a small up-front investment such as re-selling, using your car for delivery (gas), special training that can lead to part-time income. If you have the time, these types of activities can be one of the best investments. Usually the most risk is in choosing the type of activity. If you do your homework on the opportunity, talk with others who are actually doing it, this investment in yourself might offer the best risk-reward ratio.

LONG TERM GOALS (3-30 years): wealth building, retirement income, building a business, children's education.

1. **Long term investment program within a tax favored account:** Because capital gains and income taxes can reduce the net gains from investments, the government has developed a menu of special accounts that promotes developing wealth-mainly for retirement. These plans will be talked about in detail in the next chapter but for any person investing for the long term, investments should maximize the use of tax favored investment vehicles. With proper guidance from a financial professional, almost all types of investments can be positioned within a tax favored account.

2. **Annuities:** Usually provided through insurance companies, these are contracts that agree to pay a certain amount of regular income over a specific period of time dependent on the amount of money invested up front in one lump sum. This

type of investment usually has stiff penalties for early withdrawal but the risk is fairly low and the reward is about equal to a corporate bond (5-8%).

3. **Real estate:** One of the most popular long term investment made by most people and is normally represented in the form of a person's residence. You have to live somewhere and if you own your home you will build up equity over time as you pay down the loan and as property values increase. Under specific cases, the sale of a residence may also be exempt from taxes. Indeed, a home has proven to be a wise investment for most people. However, there are no guarantees.
Another popular strategy for some is to buy land for future development or to buy income generating rental properties. In fact, some investors will buy income producing properties before they purchase their own homes. These people are usually financially successful because they demonstrate the ability to forgo lifestyle for future income and equity buildup. They have control over their consumer impulse.

4. **Developing a business:** One of the best ways to build wealth. When you are an employee, you receive a wage in compensation for your work. It is steady, predictable and the risk is in losing the job. On the other hand, a business owner-developer takes the risk of losing the capital invested and any income derived from the business.

A successful business has value not only in the physical assets it owns but more so for the ability to produce income. As a result, owning a business not only provides jobs for employees, taxes for government, but also income and equity buildup for ownership. An employee builds no equity in a business because that goes to the risk-taker who put up the capital and provides the capacity to manage the company. The basic truth is: employees don't usually produce wealth from their work-only a lifestyle. Owners and investors, on the other hand, build wealth in the form of equity.

Typical Investing Model For Success

Given the fact that most people are employees, the following model applies to a wage earner who works for a company, which offers a tax deferred pension plan. However, even if you don't work for a company that has a pension plan, there are tax deferred plans available to all who work and meet certain qualifications.

The most popular employer tax favored pension plan is the 401k account. Basically, the plan allows the employee to invest up to $16,500 annually. This amount is allowed to be invested in most types of investments and gains are tax deferred until the age of retirement at which time the funds are taxed at the normal tax rate at the time the funds are withdrawn from the account. But that's not all the good news. Some company's can match (contribute) as much as the company wants up to a certain amount of funds contributed by the employee. For example, it's not uncommon for a company that wants to attract and keep top quality employees to match dollar for dollar up to the first $2,000-$4,000 deposited in the 401k by the employee. That is equivalent to a 100% return each year on the matched contributions, to say nothing of the long term compounding of gains.

 Sample Test Questions - Chapter 5

1) Financial planning consists of a mixture of _____ and _____ goals and objectives.

   A) Professional, personal
   B) Financial, professional
   C) Personal, financial
   D) Academic, personal

The correct answer is B:) Financial, professional.

2) When building a budget, one should take into account potential

   A) Surpluses
   B) Shortfalls
   C) Emergencies
   D) Liabilities

The correct answer is C:) Emergencies.

3) Life insurance for younger people is _____ in comparison with older people.

   A) More expensive
   B) Not necessary
   C) Not available
   D) Less expensive

The correct answer is D:) Less expensive.

4) Term insurance provides for _____ only.

   A) An account that pays interest on the balance
   B) A death benefit
   C) A premium
   D) A cash benefit

The correct answer is B:) A death benefit.

5) Whole life insurance provides for

   A) A cash build up of a portion of the premiums paid
   B) A cash build up of a portion of the premiums which earns interest while being accumulated
   C) A cash build up of a portion of the premium which earns interest while being accumulated and pays a death benefit
   D) A death benefit only

The correct answer is C:) A cash build up of a portion of the premium which earns interest while being accumulated and pays a death benefit. Some people feel that whole life insurance provides a way to earn passive income on premium payments while at the same time having death benefits. However, often it makes more sense to purchase a term life policy and use the difference between the whole life and term life premium and invest that separately. Buried within the whole life policy are usually additional charges and fees for management and sales commissions.

6) To begin to build wealth, you need to have an excess of _____ over _____.

   A) Income, expenses
   B) Income, required living expenses
   C) Income plus emergency funds, expenses
   D) Income, required living expenses plus emergency funds and insurance.

The correct answer is D:) Income, required living expenses plus emergency funds and insurance. Each individual will come up with how much should be allocated for potential emergencies, but some thought and resources should be allocated to the budget.

7) As a general rule, it's a good idea to have at least _____ month's living expenses immediately available.

   A) 6
   B) 3
   C) 4
   D) 12

The correct answer is C:) 4 months. This should be in a form that can be immediately liquidated. If you have investments in stocks, bonds, mutual funds or other investments that can be easily sold, these can also count for emergency funds.

8) One of today's greatest financial risks is becoming _____ without _____ insurance.

   A) Ill, disability
   B) Ill, medical
   C) Ill, term
   D) Ill, whole life

The correct answer is B:) Ill, medical. If you have assets but no medical insurance and become seriously ill and require expensive treatment, your assets can be attached for payment of medical bills.

9) Once you have made a budget and you have some extra funds, your first expense paid should be

   A) Student loan
   B) Savings and investment funds
   C) Medical insurance
   D) Entertainment

The correct answer is B:) Savings and investment funds. Set up a budget that meets the reasonable needs of your lifestyle and plan to have enough spare income to divert to emergencies and wealth building.

10) The power of _____ gains can make you a millionaire if you a disciplined program of _____.

   A) Capital, savings
   B) Compounding, spending
   C) Compounding, investing
   D) Capital, tax sheltering

The correct answer is C:) Compounding, investing. The earlier you start a disciplined program of investing, the more likely you will build wealth over the long term.

11) Financial planning is a combination of _____ , _____ and _____ .

   A) Personal planning, tax planning, financial planning
   B) Budgeting, personal planning, investment planning
   C) Goal setting, budgeting, investment planning
   D) Counseling, budgeting, investment

The correct answer is C:) Goal setting, budgeting, investment planning. Goal setting can be both personal and professional. Budgeting is the process of developing some disposable income (Income-expenses) for investing short and long term. Investment planning is finding the best form of investing to match your goals and risk profile.

12) One of the most important financial decisions a person has to make is choosing what level of _____ they can accept.

   A) Income
   B) Investing
   C) Lifestyle
   D) Saving

The correct answer is C:) Lifestyle. How you want to live your daily life will have a major impact on the expenses needed to support your lifestyle. If you have an expensive lifestyle, it will be harder to accumulate wealth in that there will be less disposable income. Indeed, meeting certain perceived lifestyle expectations has a direct effect on the ability to build wealth.

13) One of the first things you need to find out about a potential employer is if they have

   A) Sick pay
   B) Christmas bonus
   C) Term life insurance
   D) A qualified tax deferred pension plan

The correct answer is D:) A qualified tax deferred pension plan. A pension plan is the principal vehicle for long term investments because of the favorable tax protection. Also, find out how much the company matches as this is just like a tax free bonus.

14) You should not touch your pension funds because

   A) You break your discipline
   B) The company can fire you because the money is not yours until you retire
   C) The IRS can assess heavy penalties and fees
   D) You will not be eligible for company matching funds

The correct answer is C:) The IRS can assess heavy penalties and fees. Typically, if you withdraw funds from your pension fund without complying with the IRS requirements, you can be charged regular tax rate plus an additional 10%. If you were in the 35% tax bracket, you might have to pay up to 45% tax on the funds that were in your pension fund.

15) The general idea for investing is to use _____ and tax_____ to allow funds to capture the benefits of compounding _____.

   A) Mutual funds, breaks, interest
   B) Time, deferral, gains
   C) Funds, breaks, gains
   D) Time, deductions, profits

The correct answer is B:) Time, deferral, gains. The time factor urges younger people to start investing for the long term. It doesn't mean that all savings is for the long term but at least a portion should be for the long haul and not touched until retirement. Besides, the future of social security and its ability to provide a meaningful retirement is a major issue today. To a young person just starting out, thinking about retirement is a bit weird, but the important fact is that value of time starts now. For long term investing, the sooner you start the better.

16) What is churning?

   A) When a broker buys expensive stocks that their customer cannot actually afford.
   B) When a broker buys and sells stock excessively with the interests of their customer in mind.
   C) When a broker buys large amounts of stock to get a commission, even though it is unwise.
   D) None of the above

The correct answer is C:) When a broker buys large amounts of stock to get a commission, even though it is unwise. Churning can be illegal and leave the broker responsible to the customer for any losses they may have generated.

17) What is unique about a callable bond?

   A) They cannot be redeemed for at least 12 years.
   B) They have an extremely low interest rate of .05% or less.
   C) The issuer can redeem them before they are mature.
   D) None of the above

The correct answer is C:) The issuer can redeem them before they are mature.

 Chapter 6 - Retirement Plans and Estate Planning

Many people feel that they are contributing to their retirement through their Social Security contributions (FICA withholdings) and the matching of employers. However, Social Security was never intended to provide for retirement all by itself. The original intention was a post depression political maneuver make voters feel that they would have some sort of safety net, at least enough to put some food on the table. But provide for a comfortable retirement…forget about it; it was never the intention. The myth of Social Security becoming a full blown retirement plan came about during the rapid growth of the U.S. post World War II economy.

For a brief time, before the effects of price inflation kicked in-Social Security could provide a decent "widow's" pension. In today's world, the average Social Security payment is a little under $1000 per month. While Social Security benefits aren't taxed, this sum is about the average monthly food expense for a family of four. To retire on $1000 per month is a very hard thing to do in today's world. Of course, workers who have recently retired are collecting higher amounts as an effect of a longer period in the fund, but the highest amounts are a bit over $1,200 per month; still a sum well below providing for a comfortable retirement, unless you live in a tent and have a steady diet of rice and beans. However, Social Security is a nice supplement to help cover the basic cost of living during retirement.

To many, the future situation of the Social Security fund is moving into precarious territory. At the outset of the program, there were about seven workers contributing to the fund for each recipient of retirement funds. Today, there are a bit less than four workers contributing to one recipient. Given the relatively low level of returns on the fund investments (usually correlated with the 2 year Treasury bill-approx a 3% average return) the growing number of recipients are drawing down the fund faster than it can be replenished. As a result, the Social Security Fund is projected to go bankrupt by 2035. In an attempt to put a band aid on the problem, the qualifications to collect Social Security benefits have been adjusted and more tinkering is yet to come.

To draw on Social Security for retirement or disability, you must have earned credits. The credits are based on the amount of your earnings. We use your work history to determine your eligibility for retirement or disability benefits or your family's eligibility for survivors benefits when you die.

In 2011, you receive one credit for each $1,120 of earnings, up to the maximum of four credits per year.

Each year the amount of earnings needed for credits goes up slightly as average earnings levels increase. The credits you earn remain on your Social Security record even if you change jobs or have no earnings for a while.

Retirement benefits
Anyone born in 1929 or later needs 10 years of work (40 credits) to be eligible for retirement benefits. People born before 1929 need fewer years of work.

Disability benefits
How many credits you need for disability benefits depends on how old you are when you become disabled.

If you become disabled before age 24, you generally need 1½ years of work (six credits) in the three years before you became disabled.

If you are 24 through 30, you generally need credits for half of the time between age 21 and the time you became disabled.

If you are disabled at age 31 or older, you generally need at least 20 credits in the 10 years immediately before you became disabled.

Social Security reform is referred to as a political "third rail." What this means is that to touch the issue is like touching the third rail of an electric train which means instant death by electrocution; in this case, political death. Indeed, from a political point of view when congress starts playing with the income of a powerful and growing constituency such as the retired community (estimated at 40 million today and expected to double by 2050). Many plans have been offered in an attempt to be proactive in taking on this serious problem but as of yet the politicians have been successful in not touching that third rail. As a result of the political and economic realities of the situation, it is rather apparent that planning for your own retirement income makes a lot of sense. The best advice is plan for the worst and hope for the best. And that leads us nicely into our next topic of conversation: personal pension planning.

Medicaid, Medicare and Medigap are all different health care programs for elderly or disabled people. Medicare is distributed by the Health Care Financing Administration. It is essentially the same as a health care program with the government paying for some care, and the person paying for co pays and deductibles. Medicare tends to be more limited than the other two and pays for general needs. It is not a need based program. Medigap can be used to supplement Medicare. It offers more inclusive plans that may cover co payments and deductibles, but it also involves higher premiums. Medicaid is separate from the two. It is administered based on personal need and tends to pay for more skilled care such as nursing homes.

Personal Pension Planning

The basic structure of a pension plan is that of a "trust." This really means that the government doesn't trust you and because of this fact, some third party is needed to keep you from raiding your own assets. So, to make sure you don't ruin your financial future, a custodian-usually a bank or other registered financial institution- is needed to hold the pension funds and an administrator is needed to make sure the account complies with the IRS tax law. Also, most company sponsored plans have a fund manager who is responsible for making the actual investment decisions and transactions. However, what happens if you don't work for a company that offers a pension plan or you work for yourself; does that mean you are left out in the cold? Happily, the answer is no.

There are pension plans that allow just about anyone to establish their own tax favored pension plan and even to allow the account holder to act as their own funds manager. Indeed, there is a menu of pension plans to match almost any situation. Because of that, we will limit our brief discussion to the most common types of qualified tax deferred pension plans.

401k Pension Plan

If you are an employee for a company, the most typical plan many companies offer is the 401k.

A 401(k) plan is defined by the IRS as a defined contribution plan. What that means is that the employee defines a percentage of their salary they want to contribute to the plan, and the employer defines the extent of employer matching, if any. The account is established with a custodian/administrator/funds manager for the employee.

As with most tax favored plans, the employee contributions reduce the taxable wages by the amount of the contribution and goes into the employee's account where the contributions and any investment gains can accrue tax free (deferred) until time of withdrawal. In addition, an employer can choose to match a certain percentage of the employee's contributions and also contribute any bonuses or profit sharing as defined by the employer in the specific plan

- 401k loans. One of the most obvious advantages for employees who have a 401k is the ability to take out a loan from the account without penalty. Typically, the loan can be for no longer than five years and interest charged on the loan must be "reasonable." Payments need to be pre-set and mostly equal just as with a conventional loan. Employers have the latitude to make their specific plan more restrictive. However, defaulting on a 401k loan can have ugly tax consequences and it is advisable for an employee to seek tax advice before exercising this benefit.

- Contribution Limits

Total employer and employee contributions to all of an employer's plans are subject to an overall annual limitation:

Less than age 50	More than age 50
$16,500	$22,000

However, if the employer has a funds matching plan, the maximum total contribution is limited to $49,000 each year.

For example, if you are less than 50 years old and program for the company to take out the maximum contributions, you can deposit $16,500 per year in your 401k account where it can grow tax free until withdrawal. Moreover, you also deduct the $16,500 from your taxable income for the tax year. So, not only do you get to invest the $16,500 exempt from taxation, but also you avoid paying taxes on the $16,500, which if you were in the 35% tax bracket would be $5,77.50 in taxes. What a sweet deal!

The next important part of the model is that the company 401k offers a wide range of investments to allow for proper diversification of assets. For example, the plan may offer low, medium and some higher risk investments, normally mutual funds. The fund usually allows the funds to be redistributed in any fashion the employee wishes. Typically, the younger you are, the higher the percentage of higher risk investments. The company plan normally includes an investment advisor and/or the employee can use their own investment advisor.

These days because most employees do not stay with a company for their entire career, your pension plan needs to be portable. This means that if you leave the company, you get at least the funds you have contributed. Normally, any company matching funds become "vested" over a specified time with the company and become the property of the employee. For example, a company may match your contributions up to 3%. If those funds become vested after one year, then after that year, you can keep any money that was contributed. If the money is only partially vested when you leave the company, you will only get to keep a portion of the match.

The IRS has specific rules about how to transfer tax favored investments. Usually, you have 60 days to make a transfer to another tax favored plan. See a professional advisor before taking any distributions as the rules can be complex. Not to do so can place your funds at risk for penalties and fees.

So, here is a fairly common model for employees whose company offers a 401k plan. To properly take advantage of the benefits of such a plan, an employee should:

- Put as much money into the company pension plan as possible.
- Make a budget and have the company automatically deduct the investment amount you have allocated in your budget each pay period (you won't miss what you don't see).
- Make sure to find out how much the company will match and up to what point.
- Find out who the money manager is for the pension fund and learn what the manager will do with the funds under varying economic scenarios. Know when you can make adjustments to the account investments in your pension plan (usually once or twice a year).
- Learn everything about the pension plan. Read the fine print. Ask questions.
- Try not to touch your plan except for real emergencies with no other solutions. Normally, many plans will allow for tax free withdrawal under specific conditions. Learn about those conditions. Some plans even let pension funds be used for a down payment on a residence.

Consider this: you may live for a long time after you reach retirement age (maybe for as long as you have worked!) so if you want to be prepared, start planning today for tomorrow. Start early and let time and tax free compounding of gains help you slowly but surely prepare for the future. If you do it properly, your long term investing program will be painless and become a real source of pride. Particularly for younger folks, don't count on the government social security program to meet your future needs.

Individual Retirement Account - IRA

For those who work for themselves or for a company that has no pension plan to offer, each individual has the ability to open a tax favored IRA. In fact, as long as total contributions aren't exceeded, an employee can have any amount of IRAs in addition to other pension plans. Most financial institutions such as banks, mutual fund companies and brokerages can act as a custodian and administrator your IRA for a minimal fee. However, it is up to the beneficiary of the account (you) as to how the funds can be invested. Most people open up an IRA account with a mutual fund company who then act as custodian, administrator and investment manager. In fact, the particular plan normally determines the scope of investments that can be used; however according to IRs code, anything except the following can be used as an investment in an IRA:

- Life Insurance Contracts
- Collectibles such as:
    - Artwork
    - Rugs
    - Antiques
    - Metals
    - Gems
    - Stamps
    - Coins
    - Beverages (wine, etc.)
- Stock in a S-Corporation
- Other tangible personal property

Over the years, congress has adapted and created a variety of IRAs for specific purposes. Which one is best for you, will depend on many things and it is strongly suggested that deciding on what type of IRA should be part of your financial plan.

Each IRA has some special rules so it is very important to seek advice from a financial professional before setting up an IRA. However, most IRAs provide for a maximum annual contribution limit of $6,000 for individuals and $12,000 for spousal IRAs (note that a 401k allows a much higher annual maximum contribution).

Early Withdrawal from an IRA
All IRAs have a common policy regarding early withdrawal. If it is before age 59½ then funds withdrawn are subject to regular taxation plus a 10% penalty. For example, if you make an early withdrawal, you would pay your normal income tax rate plus 10%. However, if you borrow from your IRA and can replace it within 60 days, there are no penalties.

Rollover Rules
If you change employers or want to change custodians you can "roll" it into another qualified tax deferred plan. However, this transfer must be completed within 60 days from withdrawal. Again, you are urged to seek professional guidance on any rollovers or withdrawals before you take action. If you make a mistake, it can be expensive.

In summary, the main place to put your passive wealth building capital is within the numerous qualified pension plans available. However, to reap the benefits of tax protection, you must know the rules or obtain guidance from a knowledgeable financial professional.

There are protections in place for some retirement savings. The FDIC insures almost all banks and thrifts in the United States. This means that if the bank fails, each person is insured for their money up to $250,000 per account. These typically are savings and checking accounts. These are ways to keep your finances liquid. One benefit of liquid assets is that they can be quickly accessed when they are needed.

Estate Planning

For most people, wealth is not created by wages as most of that seems to go to the maintenance of lifestyle. With that in mind, using tax favored pension plans are the best vehicle for building wealth with passive income created out of disposable income. If everything goes as planned, by the time you reach retirement age or even earlier, you will have a nice lump sum of funds waiting to provide for your golden years. So, here you are with a nice lump sum as a result of a lifelong savings and investments program and then what happens if you die? In fact, what happens with your assets at anytime when you die?

When a person dies their will determines how their estate is divided among beneficiaries. First, taxes called estate taxes go to the government. Then the estate is divided according to the will. Each person who received property from the deceased person then must pay an inheritance tax to the government.

Probate is when a deceased person's assets are redistributed to pay their creditors and fulfill the terms of their will. This is the process of settling their accounts, making sure that outstanding debts are paid and that any excess is paid in the terms spelled out in the will.

For example, if you and your spouse have separate bank accounts and don't specify a beneficiary or don't set up a joint account, if you die, your spouse will be denied access to the funds in your account until release from probate proceedings, which can be months later. So, at the worst possible time, needed funds can become inaccessible. Not only that, if not set up properly, your beneficiaries might even have to pay taxes on the money in your account! By not planning, your assets can become frozen, taxed or even confiscated…and that's not including legal fees needed to free up the assets.

However, with a little thought and planning, you can make sure that your assets can pass on with little or no taxation or hang ups. Indeed, once you are dead, it's too late to do estate planning. Indeed, estate planning is just another example of proactive thinking and taking control of your life. Yes, it sounds a bit ghoulish but when you purchase something with any value, you should give it a thought; death can visit you at any time. Not only that, if you have been fortunate enough to accumulate any wealth, if you don't specify in a written document (will or other legal documents) others can lay claim to your assets. Is that what you would want to happen?

The problem with estate planning is that most people understand that we all die but they really don't believe it will happen to them! Crazy, right? Or, if you give it some consideration, it makes death become more real and we shut it out. Sometimes, estate planning is as simple as a hand written document as long as it is dated and signed by you. However, if your estate is over about $60,000 (all your assets put together), you should look for an estate attorney or financial planner who can provide you with the guidance you need. Again, this should be part of your financial planning; it's just part of doing the due diligence of a responsible person who lives in a modern, sophisticated culture.

For whatever reasons, most people would like to pass on the fruits of a lifetime without leaving loved ones to do battle with creditors, tax agents and whomever. As a result, it comes as no surprise that wealthy, sophisticated people have used their wealth and influence to pass laws that favor the protection of their estates. Indeed, when done properly, there can be little or no loss of an estate's value as protected assets pass to survivors. Why not ride their coat tails? But it takes planning with the help of a professional with special training in estate planning and taxation. Hopefully, many of you will be seeking such services in your future. What is needed to make a smooth transition of wealth to beneficiaries in a jungle of tax laws is to understand that you need professional help with this specialized knowledge. Here are the typical team members you need to gather up to help with estate planning:

- Accountant familiar with your total financial profile and assets
- An estate attorney who is familiar with estate and tax law and how to structure the complex entities (usually trusts) to minimize taxation and provide for ease of wealth transfer
- Financial advisor who is familiar with your investments-both active and passive

Yes, it costs some money to do financial and estate planning but it can cost much more not to do it.

An estate tax specifically taxes a deceased person's estate as a whole. An inheritance tax specifically taxes the people who inherit something from a deceased person and is based on what each individual receives.

If there is no benefactor listed on a life insurance policy, the money goes to the person's "estate." From there it goes to whomever the will specifies. If a person dies without having a will they are said to have died intestate.

 Sample Test Questions - Chapter 6

1) Investing should be started as _____ as possible because of the power of _____ _____.

   A) Aggressively, compounding interest
   B) Soon, compounding gains
   C) Slowly, going bust
   D) Slowly, specific knowledge

The correct answer is B:) Soon, compounding gains. Even small amounts invested regularly over time can grow exponentially because of the compounding of gains.

2) The reason that most Americans save very little of their income is because most people choose to use income as a means to sustain _____ and not create any _____.

   A) Lifestyle, savings
   B) Social class, savings
   C) Maximum gratification, discipline
   D) Lifestyle, emergency funds

The correct answer is A:) Lifestyle, savings. Lifestyle is a better word than social class because that is not clearly defined. Each person establishes in their own mind what lifestyle they aspire to. Usually, lifestyle is greatly influenced by how one has been raised. One of the best strategies is to accept a lower lifestyle for a period of time and create savings to be able to invest and then establish lifestyle (this is called "deferred gratification"). Most people do it in reverse ("instant gratification").

3) A person should maximize investments in qualified pension plans because of

   A) Low management fees
   B) Professional management
   C) Tax exemption
   D) Tax deferral

The correct answer is D:) Tax deferral. When reaching the age of eligibility for withdrawals, taxes are paid at the person's tax rate at the time of withdrawal. Before withdrawal, all gains are protected from taxes and this allows for higher total gains on the investments.

4) The basic structure of a qualified pension plan is that of a

    A) Mutual fund
    B) Savings account
    C) Trust
    D) 401k

The correct answer is C:) Trust. A trust is set up to supposedly keep the beneficiary from abusing the favorable tax laws. Typically, there is a custodial, administrator and investment management.

5) Is it true that only a company can establish a qualified pension plan?

    A) Yes
    B) No

The correct answer is B:) No. Individuals can established a qualified pension plan by setting up an Individual Retirement Account (IRA).

6) If your employer provides a 401k pension plan, one of the most important things to look for is if the company has a _____ program.

    A) Savings
    B) Trust
    C) Mutual fund
    D) Matching

The correct answer is D:) Matching. Some companies try to attract and keep employees by offering a matching funds program whereby the employer will match dollar for dollar any employee contributions to their 401k plans. Indeed, this equates to a 100% guaranteed return for the employee on the matching funds.

7) Not only do you get to contribute tax deferred funds to your qualified pension plan but you also can _____ the contributions from _____ income.

    A) Invest, interest
    B) Deduct, passive
    C) Deduct, taxable
    D) Deposit, savings

The correct answer is C:) Deduct, taxable. This is a double benefit because the contribution deducted can put you in a lower tax bracket for your taxable income.

8) If you need money from your IRA account, you will be required to

   A) Write a letter to the IRS explaining the reasons why you need the money
   B) Pay a commission to the custodian
   C) Return the money within 120 days
   D) Pay income taxes plus a 10% penalty on the funds withdrawn

The correct answer is D:) Pay income taxes plus a 10% penalty on the funds withdrawn.

9) If you are single and younger than 50 years old, for a 401k plan, the maximum annual unmatched contribution is_____ and the maximum for an IRA annual contribution is_____.

   A) $6,000, $16,500
   B) $16,500, $6,000
   C) $10,000, $10,000
   D) $22,000, $12,000

The correct answer is B:) $16,500, $6,000.

10) Because the government doesn't trust the beneficiary to make wise investment decisions, all pension funds must have a professional investment manager.

   A) True
   B) False

The correct answer is B:) False. It is possible for the beneficiary of many pension plans to establish a self directed plan whereby the beneficiary can choose the investments but a custodian and administrator are still required.

11) The main purpose for estate planning is to

   A) Avoid paying income taxes
   B) Minimize estate taxes
   C) Make sure assets are transferred with the fewest potential problems
   D) To register assets with the government

The correct answer is C:) Make sure assets are transferred with the fewest potential problems. If there are no clear instructions from the owner of assets as to the transfer of assets after death can lead to probate, legal and estate tax problems.

12) You open a savings account and later you die. You have no will and the account was not a joint account. Who would most likely get the savings account?

   A) The oldest member of your immediate family
   B) Your pet hamster
   C) The bank
   D) Anyone who wants to claim it

The correct answer is D:) Anyone who wants to claim it. Although this would happen after a legal waiting period, if there is no will, joint tenant or beneficiary, anyone can claim the account. Of course, the claim could be contested, either way, it would most likely require the costs of legal representation and could be subject to probate taxes.

13) If you wanted to purchase income producing real estate within a tax deferred account, you could set up a

   A) Real estate company
   B) Trust account
   C) 401k
   D) Real estate IRA

The correct answer is D:) Real estate IRA. There are many types of IRAs and a person can own multiple IRAs. However, there are specific requirements for each type of IRA account and it is important to know all aspects before funding the account. For example, a real estate IRA does not allow you to purchase a primary residence with IRA funds.

14) Under certain specific conditions, IRA funds can be withdrawn without penalties.

   A) True
   B) False

The correct answer is A:) True. Most IRAs provide for funds withdrawal without penalties if the funds are replaced within 60 days. Also, under some emergency situations, such as illness, can allow for penalty free withdrawal. However, as with all qualified pension plans, each situation needs to be examined closely for compliance.

15) Generally speaking, when you move funds from one qualified pension plan to another within _____ days, this is referred to as a _____.

   A) 45, transfer of pension funds
   B) 60, job change provision
   C) 60, rollover
   D) 30, pension transfer

The correct answer is C:) 60, rollover. There can be a direct transfer from one plan to another or a rollover where one account is cashed out and then re deposited into another qualified plan within 60 days. Failing to comply with all specific requirements can trigger taxes and fees.

16) What does it mean if a will is probated?

   A) It is accepted as genuine and valid.
   B) It is executed and the inheritors are given their inheritance.
   C) It is determined that it is not valid because the testator was not sane.
   D) None of the above

The correct answer is A:) It is accepted as genuine and valid. This is determined by a probate court. A will could be denied probate if the testator can be proven to have been under influence or mentally incapable of making proper decisions.

17) Which of the following best describes a difference between a will and a trust?

   A) A will determines the disposal of a person's estate after they die. A trust operates while they are alive and after they die.
   B) Estate taxes only have to be paid on a will; otherwise they operates fairly similarly.
   C) A trust determines the disposal of a person's estate after they die. A will operates while they are alive and after they die.
   D) There is no difference between a will and a trust.

The correct answer is A:) A will determines the disposal of a person's estate after they die. A trust operates while they are alive and after they die.

18) What does it mean if a person dies intestate?

    A) They had made a will before they died.
    B) They died without completing a will.
    C) They were not citizens when they died, and therefore no estate tax must be paid on their estate.
    D) None of the above.

The correct answer is B:) They died without completing a will.

19) What does the FDIC insure?

    A) Mortgages
    B) Stocks
    C) Cars
    D) Bank accounts

The correct answer is D:) Bank accounts. The FDIC insures for up to $250,000.

Sample Test Questions - Overview

1) Which of the following BEST describes Medigap?

   A) A supplemental insurance plan that helps pay for costs that aren't covered by Medicare.
   B) A gap in the coverage offered by Medicare that excludes many people from full coverage.
   C) A new insurance plan that replaces Medicare for a plan with more complete coverage.
   D) A primary insurance plan that Medicare is supplemental to.

The correct answer is A:) A supplemental insurance plan that helps pay for costs that aren't covered by Medicare. For example, international expenses, co-payments, deductibles, and fees associated with Medicare can be covered by Medigap coverage plans. Medigap plans are purchased from a private insurance company and require a monthly premium payment.

2) An SEP is similar to which of the following?

   A) Medicare
   B) IRA
   C) Passbook savings account
   D) None of the above.

The correct answer is B:) IRA. An SEP, or Simplified Employee Pension Plan, is an IRA based pension plan that is typically used by small businesses with few employees. It allows tax-deductible contributions of up to 25% of an employee's income to be made, but is simpler to manage than a normal IRA.

3) Wages and taxes withheld for the year are reported on which form?

   A) Schedule SE
   B) I-9
   C) W-4
   D) W-2

The correct answer is D:) W-2. The W-2 form is completed by an employer and given to an employee so that they can correctly fill out their tax forms each year. It includes information such as wages or salary for the year, federal taxes withheld, and local taxes withheld.

4) Before electronic banking was available, what type of book was used to allow accountholders to have access to their deposit and account information?

   A) Surplus book
   B) Blue book
   C) Passbook
   D) Dual-account ledger

The correct answer is C:) Passbook. A passbook was approximately the size of a passport or checkbook, and was passed between the account holder and the teller each time a transaction was made so that each party could keep a record of the transactions. Prior to the introduction of passbooks, the information was stored only on the bank's ledgers, and account holders did not have regular access to the information.

5) Which stock exchange is known for having a higher quantity of technology companies?

   A) FDIC
   B) NASDAQ
   C) Chicago Mercantile Exchange
   D) NYSE

The correct answer is D:) NYSE. The two largest stock exchanges in the United States are the NASDAQ and the NYSE. Of the two, the NYSE has a reputation for listing technology, internet, and start-up companies. The NASDAQ, on the other hand, is known for listing more stable and mature companies.

6) Amber completes her will shortly before her death. She leaves the majority of her wealth to her daughter Ashley and her son Jonathan. Her attorney Matthew is responsible for ensuring the will is properly executed. In this situation, who is the decedent?

   A) Amber
   B) Ashley
   C) Jonathan
   D) Matthew

The correct answer is A:) Amber. A decedent is a person who has died. The purpose of the will is to ensure that the decedent's assets are managed in the way that the individual would want them to be.

7) A person who has made a valid will is known as a(n)

   A) Testator
   B) Codicil
   C) Residual author
   D) Agent

The correct answer is A:) Testator. Although the term testator can refer to a male or female who has written a will, the term testatrix is occasionally used for women.

8) A codicil is

   A) A statute in the tax code
   B) An individual who benefits from a will
   C) A document that amends a will
   D) A contribution to a retirement account

The correct answer is C:) A document that amends a will. A codicil is any document that legally amends or alters a will in any way. The benefit of a codicil is that it does not require that the entire will be invalidated for a simple change to be made.

9) Jonathan decides to lease a car. If he were to buy the car new it would have a value of $35,000, but he only has to make monthly payments of $350. The dealership expects that the value of the car at the end of the 5-year lease will be $20,000. What is the residual value of the car?

   A) $350
   B) $15,000
   C) $20,000
   D) $35,000

The correct answer is C:) $20,000. The residual value of the car is the amount that it will be worth once the lease is completed. In this situation, that amount is stated as $20,000.

10) A W-4 form is to be filled out by the

   A) Employer
   B) Employee
   C) Government
   D) More than one of the above

The correct answer is B:) Employee. The W-4 is a form that employees fill out to inform their employer about their tax status. Employers use the form to determine the amount of taxes that they should withhold from each paycheck.

11) A mortgage that has movable property as collateral is known as a

   A) Chattel mortgage
   B) Loose collateral mortgage
   C) Uninsured mortgage
   D) Umbrella mortgage

The correct answer is A:) Chattel mortgage. Traditionally a mortgage is collateralized by the actual property. In some circumstances, however, the mortgage may use other property or movable property as collateral. For example, a mobile home would be considered chattel mortgage because it is not stationary throughout the period of the mortgage.

12) Which of the following is NOT typically covered under homeowners insurance?

   A) Structure of the house
   B) Personal belongings
   C) Liability protection
   D) All of the above are generally included in homeowners insurance.

The correct answer is D:) All of the above are generally included in homeowners insurance. In addition to these three aspects of homeowners insurance, many policies will also cover a certain amount of additional living expenses if for some reason the home is temporarily uninhabitable.

13) Who is responsible for paying unemployment insurance?

   A) Employees
   B) Employers
   C) Government agencies
   D) Both A and B

The correct answer is B:) Employers. Due to the Federal Unemployment Tax Act all employers are responsible to pay unemployment tax for their employees. This funds the unemployment program that allows the government to give unemployment tax to individuals who lose their jobs.

14) Marketing and distribution fees for mutual funds are known as

   A) Normal operations fees
   B) Umbrella fees
   C) Surplus fees
   D) 12b-1 fees

The correct answer is D:) 12b-1 fees. Although such fees were originally meant to help mutual funds operate more efficiently, their continued relevance is often questioned. Sometimes they become a way of paying commissions or premiums to brokers. The fees are paid out throughout the year.

15) An umbrella insurance policy is

   A) A supplemental insurance plan that helps pay for costs that aren't covered by Medicare
   B) An insurance policy that helps facilitate coverage when both your house and car are involved
   C) An insurance policy that covers you in a lawsuit when regular liability insurance isn't enough
   D) A policy that targets coverage for natural disasters that you only pay if you need to use it

The correct answer is C:) An insurance policy that covers you in a lawsuit when regular liability insurance isn't enough. Typically, umbrella policies will start at one million dollars and are used to supplement costs that exceed the amount of your liability coverage.

16) Janet earns a yearly salary of $35,000. She pays taxes each year of $12,250 leaving her with $22,750. Her allowable income before surplus each month is $1,950. Based on these facts, $22,750 is Janet's

A) Gross income
B) Net income
C) Surplus income
D) Taxable income

The correct answer is B:) Net income. Janet's gross income would be $35,000, or the amount that she earns before any taxes have been taken out. Her net income is the amount that she makes after paying taxes.

17) Uninsured motorist clauses in insurance policies

A) Require your insurance to pay for damages if you are injured by an uninsured individual
B) Require that an uninsured individual obtain insurance if they are involved in an accident
C) Free the insurance company from any liability if you are injured by an uninsured individual
D) None of the above

The correct answer is A:) Require your insurance to pay for damages if you are injured by an uninsured individual. Uninsured motorist clauses are commonly found in car insurance policies, although they may cost an additional premium.

 Test Taking Strategies

Here are some test-taking strategies that are specific to this test and to other DSST tests in general:

- Keep your eyes on the time. Pay attention to how much time you have left.
- Read the entire question and read all the answers. Many questions are not as hard to answer as they may seem. Sometimes, a difficult sounding question really only is asking you how to read an accompanying chart. Chart and graph questions are on most DANTES/DSST tests and should be an easy free point.
- If you don't know the answer immediately, the new computer-based testing lets you mark questions and come back to them later if you have time.
- Read the wording carefully. Some words can give you hints to the right answer. There are no exceptions to an answer when there are words in the question such as always, all or none. If one of the answer choices includes most or some of the right answers, but not all, then that is not the answer. Here is an example:

    The primary colors include all of the following:
    A) Red, Yellow, Blue, Green
    B) Red, Green, Yellow
    C) Red, Orange, Yellow
    D) Red, Yellow, Blue

    Although item A includes all the right answers, it also includes an incorrect answer, making it incorrect. If you didn't read it carefully, were in a hurry, or didn't know the material well, you might fall for this.

- Make a guess on a question that you do not know the answer to. There is no penalty for an incorrect answer. Eliminate the answer choices that you know are incorrect. For example, this will let your guess be a 1 in 3 chance instead.

 Test Preparation

How much you need to study depends on your knowledge of a subject area. If you are interested in literature, took it in school, or enjoy reading then your study and preparation for the literature or humanities test will not need to be as intensive as that of someone who is new to literature.

This book is much different than the regular DANTES study guides. This book actually teaches you the information that you need to know to pass the test. If you are particularly interested in an area, or feel that you want more information, do a quick search online. We've tried not to include too much depth in areas that are not as essential on the test. Everything in this book will be on the test. It is important to understand all major theories and concepts listed in the table of contents. It is also important to know any bolded words.

Don't worry if you do not understand or know a lot about the area. With minimal study, you can complete and pass the test.

One of the fallacies of other test books is test questions. People assume that the content of the questions are similar to what will be on the test. That is not the case. They are only there to test your "test taking skills" so for those who know to read a question carefully, there is not much added value from taking a "fake" test.

To prepare for the test, make a series of goals. Allot a certain amount of time to review the information you have already studied and to learn additional material. Take notes as you study; it will help you learn the material.

Legal Note

All rights reserved. This Study Guide, Book and Flashcards are protected under US Copyright Law. No part of this book or study guide or flashcards may be reproduced, distributed or stored in a retrieval system, or transmitted in any form or by any means, electronic, mechanical, photocopying, recording, or otherwise, without the prior written permission of the publisher Breely Crush Publishing, LLC.

DSST is a registered trademark of The Thomson Corporation and its affiliated companies, and does not endorse this book.

FLASHCARDS

This section contains flashcards for you to use to further your understanding of the material and test yourself on important concepts, names or dates. Read the term or question then flip the page over to check the answer on the back. Keep in mind that this information may not be covered in the text of the study guide. Take your time to study the flashcards, you will need to know and understand these concepts to pass the test.

Nominal Interest	**CPI**
Market basket	**TVM**
GDP	**Employment Cost Index**
Index of Leading Economic Indicators	**Fed Funds Rate**

Consumer Price Index	Stated interest rate
Time Value of Money	Goods that are representative of the normal purchases in the local economy
Monitor inflation by measuring changes in labor costs for money wages and salaries	Gross Domestic Product
The interest rate the Central Bank charges member banks for borrow overnight funds	11 economic reports, such as initial unemployment claims, stock market activity, etc.

Secured Credit	What kind of credit is a credit card?
How many years does something stay on your credit?	Chapter 13
Chapter 7	FSBO
Fixed rate	Adjustable rate

Unsecured credit	A loan backed by collateral
Bankruptcy where you pay some or all of your debt back	7
For sale by owner	Bankruptcy where all your debts are discharged without any re-payments
An initial lower rate than that of the fixed rate but that rate is adjusted after a specified time	When a loan is "locked in" at a certain interest rate for the duration of the loan

Upside down	Another name for "discount rate"
PV	W-2
W-4	W-9
1099	FICA

Interest rate	When you owe more on the vehicle than it is worth
A statement that shows how much money you made in a year and any withholdings from your check	Present value
A form filled out where you provide your name, address, and SSN. Used mainly for independent contractors	A form filled out where you state your exemptions to determine the correct amount of tax to be withheld
Federal Insurance Contributions Act - a withholding tax	The equivalent of a W-2 but for independent contractors

Hedging inflation	A FICO score rates your what?
APR	FOMC
What are the three major credit bureaus?	Front loaded interest
At what age can you withdraw from your IRA and not have a penalty?	CD

Credit	Preserving the value of money over time
Federal Open Market Committee	Annual percentage rate
The first five years or so almost the entire monthly payment is composed of just interest with little reduction in the principle of the loan	Experian, Equifax and Trans Union
Certificate of Deposit	59.5

Collateralized Debt	**EBIT**
529 Plan	**Bear market**
Points on a loan	**A schedule of financial activity**
Bull market	**401k**

Earnings before interest and taxes	Something tangible that is held as a guarantee against a debt
When a market is in decline	An education savings plan where money is taken out of your check tax free
Budget	Percentage rate
Savings plan	When the market is going up

IRS	IRA
Diversification	Term life insurance
Whole life insurance	What date do you have to file your personal taxes by?
You must file a tax return if you make over	Sallie Mae

Retirement savings plan	Internal Revenue Service
Includes death benefit only	Having different types of investments
April 15th	Covers death benefit and includes a interest bearing savings account
Student loan provider	$500 per year

www.ingramcontent.com/pod-product-compliance
Lightning Source LLC
Chambersburg PA
CBHW081832300426
44116CB00014B/2556